Praise for Ellen
Her Powerful—and empowering—
Relationship Guides

"Ellen Sue Stern offers women a spiritual guide for accepting their partner while including practical strategies for getting what they need as well."
>—John Gray, Ph.D., best-selling author of
>*Men Are from Mars, Women Are from Venus*

"*Loving an Imperfect Man* can help you take the pains of your life and turn them into labor pains—labor pains that help you give birth to yourself and a new life."
>—Bernie Siegel, M.D., author of
>*Love, Medicine and Miracles*

"Every married woman or prospective bride needs to read this book . . . because there is no such thing as a perfect man . . . every woman who loves a man is in the same boat—*Loving an Imperfect Man*. When you accept that, and decide to fall in love with yourself, you will have fewer ulcers, divorces, and more happiness. 'Loving ourselves is the key to loving and living with an imperfect man. That's what this book is all about.'"
>—*The Pilot* (Southern Pines, NC)

"Homespun advice from women prone to putting themselves last on a long list of people needing their time and attention. . . . Stern speaks from that place where Mom sits down at the kitchen table to talk about men and life with her daughters, or where women lean over the back fence (or the cappuccino) to discuss intimate relationships. With personal stories drawn from her own and other women's lives, Stern holds up to the light both foolish mistakes and wiser choices and concludes that, by approaching self-care and relationships differently, men and women can and should learn a great deal from one another."
>—*Publishers Weekly*

BOOKS BY ELLEN SUE STERN

The Indispensable Woman: You're the Hardest Worker, the Best Wife, Best Mother, Best Friend. But What Is It Doing to You?
Running on Empty: Meditations for Indispensable Women
Expecting Change: The Emotional Journey Through Pregnancy
I Do: Meditations for Brides
I'm Having a Baby: Meditations for Expectant Mothers
I'm a Mom: Meditations for New Mothers
In My Prime: Meditations for Women in Midlife
Starting Over: Meditations for Divorced Women
Living with Loss: Meditations for Grieving Widows
Questions Kids Wish They Could Ask Their Parents (with Zoe Stern)
Divorce Is Not the End of the World (with Zoe and Evan Stern)
Loving an Imperfect Man
He Just Doesn't Get It: Simple Solutions to the Most Common Relationship Problems

He Just Doesn't Get It!

Simple Solutions to the Most Common Relationship Problems

ELLEN SUE STERN

POCKET BOOKS

New York London Toronto Sydney Tokyo Singapore

An *Original* Publication of POCKET BOOKS

POCKET BOOKS, a division of Simon & Schuster Inc.
1230 Avenue of the Americas, New York, NY 10020

Library of Congress Cataloging-in-Publication Data:

Stern, Ellen Sue, 1954–
  He just doesn't get it! : simple solutions to the most common relationship problems / Ellen Sue Stern.
    p. cm.
ISBN: 0-671-52515-8
  1. Interpersonal conflict. 2. Intimacy (Psychology) 3. Man-woman
relationships. I. Title.
BF637.I4S74 1999
306.7—dc21   98-31372
                                                          CIP

First Pocket Books trade paperback printing January 1999

10 9 8 7 6 5 4 3 2 1

POCKET and colophon are registered trademarks of
Simon & Schuster Inc.

Cover design by Brigid Pearson

Printed in the U.S.A.

This book is dedicated in loving memory
to
Macey Orman Roiblatt Schick.

ACKNOWLEDGMENTS

Numerous friends, family members, and colleagues have been a tremendous source of love and encouragement throughout the writing of this book. I want especially to thank the following individuals: my parents, Frank and Rosalie Kiperstin; my children, Zoe and Evan Stern; Faith and Carl Schway; Jill Edelstein; Rita Magnan; Joseph Morris; Martha Morris; Michael Gorsky; Carol Wicker; Scott Stevenson; Erin Swenson; Bonnie Dickel Hoffman; and Joel Hodroff. A special thanks to Amy Pierpont for her collaborative spirit and excellent editing; Beverly Lewis, for continuing to help me sort through my ideas; and all of Zoe's friends, who keep me feeling young and willing to fall in love again.

CONTENTS

INTRODUCTION   1

1 If he doesn't understand why you're
   reading this book (or "get" all the
   ways in which you try to strengthen
   your relationship)   17

2 If he doesn't do his share   32

3 If he says, "Stop acting like
   my mother!"   44

4 If he takes you for granted   55

5 If he says he wants space   73

6 If he doesn't take your needs, time,
   and schedule into consideration   84

7 If he's more about having sex than
   about making love   101

Contents

8 If he acts as if he deserves a medal
for doing what you do twenty-four
hours a day   115

9 If he accuses you of being
high-maintenance   125

10 If he isn't supportive of or involved
in your career, interests,
or hobbies   135

11 If he mysteriously disappears when
it's time for the kids' bath (or fails
to take responsibility for other
familial, social, or community
involvement)   155

12 If he has a three-minute attention
span when talking about feelings   176

13 If he breaks promises faster than
he makes them   193

14 If he doesn't treat you well   207

15 If he doesn't make your relationship
enough of a priority   220

AND ONE FOR GOOD LUCK: If he doesn't
say "I love you" enough   232

AFTERWORD   240

He
Just
Doesn't
Get
It!

INTRODUCTION

T rue confession: I wish I were writing a different book. I'd love to call it HERE'S WHAT SHE WANTS: *Simple Ways to Satisfy the Woman You Love.* Or, WHAT A GUY! *Fifteen Ways in Which Men Are Sensitive, Loving, and Generous.*

My first choice is out of the question because, according to research, men don't buy many self-help books. What this actually means is that men don't make the same effort women do to please their mate and improve their intimate relationship. And they're not about to start, no matter what I call the book or how much men could learn from reading it.

Although I could easily write the second book—including chapters with titles such as "If he always comments on how nice you look," "If he is a totally involved father," "If he consistently initiates deep conversations about intimacy," "If he tells you to go read a book while he puts the kids to bed," "If he holds you when you're crying," and "If he listens to your feelings without telling you what to do"—it would never sell. Why? Because it would consist of one page with the single sentence "Thank you, God, for giving me the man of my dreams," and that would be the end of the book.

I can't wait to write the second book. I hope that someday we will all feel that way about the man in our life. Meanwhile most of us still have a ways to go. Of course, this doesn't keep the majority of women, including myself, from choosing men as our primary partner.

Personally, I happen to adore men. Despite a couple of marriages and enough relationships to make me gun-shy, if not downright cynical, I still am drawn to and fall in love with men. I can't help it. Maybe it's just plain old chemistry, a primal, lust-driven, endorphin-based animal attraction to their brute strength, hard bodies, and those ripples in their shoulders. Or maybe it's the challenge of finding the right balance between gently extricating their soft, tender side while pushing through their tough, macho resistance—sort of an emotional tug-of-war that appeals to my need for drama, tension, and female "conquest," if you will. In short, I haven't given up on men. If anything, the older I get, the more determined I am to crack the age-old male-female dilemma.

Both personally and professionally in my work with women, through writing thirteen self-help books, counseling, and conducting relationship seminars, I've devoted the past decade to unraveling the perpetual mystery of what makes men tick and how we can live with them more easily. The fact is that men are maddening. They can be stubborn, difficult, even impossibly frustrating when it comes to meeting some of our deepest longings and desires. By the same token, they can also be incredibly wonderful. Our partners have numerous redeeming qualities, or we wouldn't be with them in the first place. Still, even those women who give their relationship relatively high marks complain of being somewhat dissatisfied with their partner. Bottom line: after years of "working on their relationships," the majority of women still sigh, shake their head, shrug their shoulders, and recite what's become the buzz phrase of the nineties: *He just doesn't get it.*

The first ten times I heard ten different women say, "He just doesn't get it," I nodded my head in sympathy and agreement, thinking, Now those are the truest five words in the English language. The next hundred times I heard the exact same line from friends, coworkers, casual acquaintances, women in my workshops, the girl behind the counter at the dry cleaners, even my fifteen-year-old daughter, and, yes, out of my own mouth, I decided it was a fad, the sisterhood slogan / Girl Scout motto we've adopted en masse.

Why do we say it? Because it's true. Men don't get it. But guess what? Neither do we! After spending more than a decade encouraging women to accept, accommodate, or find strategies to cope with this seemingly irrevocable reality, I've come to this startling revelation. I've realized that if anything's going to improve, we, as women, have to get one thing straight: he doesn't get it. He may or may not ever get it, at least in ways that make a dramatic and lasting change in the quality of our relationship. Meanwhile we're wasting precious time and energy trying to get him to get it, when we'd be better off facing reality, or in other words—seeing him as he really is so that we can have the best possible relationship with the man we love.

And we each do love our partner. But let's be honest. If you're like most other women, you spend far too much of your time wishing your partner would change and trying to improve your relationship. Over the years you may have tried any or all of the following: counseling, support groups, relationship seminars, self-help books, comparing notes with friends, seeking New Age perspectives, tuning in to Dr. Laura, turning on the *Oprah Winfrey Show,* and, most of all, focusing your energies on figuring out how to accept, deal with, and resolve the particular issues that get in the way of having the relationship you want.

Aren't you getting tired of working that hard? Something's wrong here. Relationships have become far too complicated and fraught with struggle, which somehow we've come to accept as the norm. It's as if an entire generation has been brainwashed into thinking that intimate relationships, by definition, are 90 percent work and only 10 percent pleasure and joy. Instead of being fun, romantic, sexy, and loving, our relationships have become full-time jobs. We're spending far too much time processing issues when we could be increasing our enjoyment and appreciation of each other.

Don't get me wrong. Every relationship has its share of conflicts and issues, the obvious result of two individual human beings trying to combine their lives. None of us has the perfect relationship. There's no perfect man (at least, not once we've passed the initial courtship period). Everyone makes trade-offs; most women have at least one or more things they wish they could change about their partner, and this keeps them from enjoying their relationship to the fullest.

Since no two men are alike, no two men share exactly the same "limitations" or positive attributes. The purpose of this book is for you to learn more about the particular man in your life so that you can improve what's lacking and maximize what's working well in your relationship. Because, for better or worse, your partner comes with both wonderful gifts and aggravating problems—just as you do.

That's not to say that counseling, seminars, and other therapeutic venues aren't helpful. They can be, and often they result in profound long-term changes. But these changes take time, and they may or may not yield permanent change. Couples who enter into intensive counseling may discover that this process often resembles the myth of Sisyphus, where you take one step forward but then two steps back. Typically, some things may change a little, some behavior may improve temporarily, then our partner regresses, and we're back to the drawing board. Couples counseling can result in permanent psychological shifts, but the process is expensive and time-consuming. Meanwhile, we're not getting any younger. Life is too short to keep struggling so hard, spinning our wheels and burning up our brain cells trying to come up with the magic formula to get our mate to be who we want him to be.

It doesn't work, and it isn't ever going to work. So where does this leave us? If we can't get our partner to change through the multitude of methods we've tried, how do we stop being angry and start getting more of what we want in our relationship?

What works are *behavioral changes*—altering our own actions and approach so as to create more immediate, tangible results. It shouldn't take twenty years and thousands of dollars in therapy to have a satisfying relationship with someone you love. On the other hand, making behavioral changes doesn't mean that we stop processing feelings, and it definitely doesn't mean that we should let our part-

5

ner off the hook. It simply means getting real about who he is, what is and isn't possible to change, and then taking a more strategic approach to problem solving.

This perspective represents a dramatic departure from what I've advocated in the past. For the past twelve years my work has focused on the deep, psychological underpinnings in male-female relationships. I've always put the highest value on feelings, believing that if we can understand, accept, and express our feelings, we can get beyond our pain and create healthier relationships. Although I'm still fascinated with the psychological dynamics present in intimate relationships, I've come to believe that appealing to men on an emotional level isn't the be-all and end-all. It's effective with our women friends, but men, in general, are far more responsive to a behavioral approach. One woman put it perfectly: "They need a flowchart. You'd be amazed at how much better things work if you just give them explicit directions and tell them exactly what to do and how to do it."

I've also come to believe that hashing and rehashing past wounds has its limits. Maybe I'm just tired of listening to men defend their behavior by explaining how hurt they were in childhood. When it comes right down to it, all that really matters is behavior. Most of us have been wounded in one way or another, but that doesn't entitle us to stay stuck in the past or permit unacceptable behavior in the present. After a while it's tempting to say, "Grow up!" or "Get over it and get on with your life!" There comes a point when it just doesn't matter whether his mother toilet trained him too early or his first love dumped him for his best friend or his father was a tyrant or he was dyslexic in third grade, or . . . or . . .

Which, of course, is exactly what hooks us. Women tend

to be highly empathetic, which makes it easy to get pulled into our partner's emotional drama (and excuses) and think that we can save him, heal him, and love him into loving himself so that he'll become the man we know he can be.

Forget it. This may sound harsh and it may sound patronizing toward men, but it's critical to stop getting caught up in our mate's emotional drama and start paying more attention to what *we* need in order to improve our relationship.

How do we do this? First, we start by expecting more from our mate. No matter how much emotional baggage he's brought into the relationship, we must stop justifying his shortcomings and start expecting him to act like a responsible adult. One casualty of the New Age self-help movement has been the propensity of individuals to abdicate personal responsibility, especially in the arena of intimate relationships. Understanding the patterns created in our childhood is useful information, but blaming our parents for our adult behavior is a way of remaining stuck. At some point it's simply time to let the past be the past and move on. Similarly, New Age doctrine has perpetuated a subtle yet powerful message that any and all behavior is acceptable and above reproach, which is a dangerous stance. To be loving, accepting, and nonjudgmental is an admirable goal, but there's a point at which we have to insist on a certain standard of acceptable behavior within our intimate relationship. When we buy into the "I don't want to pressure you to do anything that doesn't feel right" attitude, we inadvertently weaken our position and give our partner permission to slack off.

Male bashing is a good example of this. It may be true, and it may be our coping mechanism for blowing off steam and a way of bonding with other women, but it's getting stale. And in a convoluted way, male bashing just serves to excuse men's behavior. We can keep shrugging our shoulders, rolling our eyes, and commiserating with our friends about how "men just don't get it," *or* we can figure out concrete ways to decrease our frustration and increase our level of satisfaction so that we can, once and for all, learn how to create a successful, lasting relationship.

That's what we *really* want. Despite how confusing, difficult, and infuriating men can be, the fact is, if you're reading this book, it's because you want to be happier with the man in your life. How? It's fairly simple. This book contains solutions to the fifteen most common relationship problems women experience with men. I hate to generalize, since I can find an exception to every rule. For example, I know plenty of men who are emotionally responsive and actively engaged in improving their relationship. But the nature of this book requires talking about men as a group (tribe, species, choose whatever word works for you). Obviously every issue addressed in this book doesn't apply to every relationship. Some women are involved with men who are incredibly devoted fathers but are weak in the romance department. Some men are emotionally supportive but never pick up their socks, some are great lovers but lousy at making a living. Take what applies to you and disregard the rest.

In a similar vein, not every relationship involves the same degree of struggle and conflict. Some women have relatively minor complaints about their partner, some are chronically angry or disappointed, and some are at the point of questioning whether this is the right man for them. But whether you're in a relationship that's seriously on the rocks or one that involves only a few chronic issues or minor complaints that get in the way, the strategies in this book will help you to permanently improve the quality of your relationship.

So how do we turn our relationship around without spending years in therapy? The place to start is by accepting four basic facts.

Fact Number 1: You Chose Him. Now he may not have turned out to be exactly what you expected (you're probably not exactly what he expected, either!), but here's a reality check: If you're with him now and continuing to be with him for the time being, that's your choice and you need to take responsibility for it.

Taking responsibility requires facing the tough issues as well as recognizing the positive aspects of your relationship. If you've picked up this book, then you're surely aware of what's missing in your relationship. But it's equally important to focus on what is working. Before you begin reading the following chapters, take a moment—five minutes, fifteen minutes, a half hour or however long it takes—to think of at least *four good reasons* for being in your relationship. This is a prerequisite for reading this book. Why? Because unless you can identify your positive reasons for being with your partner, you won't have the necessary motivations to try the strategies presented in this book.

Note: Your reasons for being in your relationship are valid, no matter what they are. You may be madly in love, you may be comfortable, even if the passion has dissipated, or at this stage of the game you may have a good "working relationship" that is more like being roommates than romantic partners. You may have made certain compromises, you may vacillate between feeling frustrated and feeling okay about where things are, or you may be in a "wait and see" mode. Your reasons for staying may be based on honoring your vows, on the commitment to raise children together, on financial considerations, or on your fear of being alone and/or of having to start over with someone else.

Don't judge your reasons for being in your relationship. There are no good or bad reasons, unless you're in an abusive relationship, in which case you need a therapist or lawyer instead of this book. Otherwise, what is, is. You needn't defend your reasons to anyone, nor compare your relationship to anyone else's. You do, however, have to be honest with yourself. Just be conscious of whatever is keeping you in your relationship, no matter what it is.

Knowing *why* you're with your partner is important because it's the key to stop blaming him or feeling like a victim. As you read on, constantly keep these reasons in the forefront of your mind; they're the fuel that keeps you going and inspires you to do what it takes to have a better relationship despite your differences, which are partly due to Fact Number 2:

Fact Number 2: HE'S A GUY.   Even though I believe that underneath it all, women and men are essentially human beings, with the same basic needs, desires, fears, and foibles, I've come to the conclusion that men do seem to share a number of universal qualities (and/or limitations) that drive women nuts.

Is it nature or nurture? Were they born that way or were they raised that way? It doesn't really matter. What's true is that thousands, maybe millions, of strikingly dissimilar women describe their relationship issues in such eerily similar terms that after a while it starts to sound as if every woman out there is involved with the very same man. The name, the appearance, the career, the country, may change, but when it comes right down to it, woman after woman says some or all of the following about her partner: "Why are men so selfish?" "How can they be so oblivious?" "Are men intimacy impaired?" "Will he ever grow up?" And, perhaps most important of all, "Will he ever understand me and love me in the way I long to be loved?"

As much as I resist the idea that we're aliens from different planets, I have to admit that there's something going on here. Thousands of women can't be experiencing the same things without there being some truth to the idea that women and men operate differently, which can be comforting, especially at those times when you stare at your partner in utter disbelief, wondering if he's truly from outer space.

He's not. Although he may seem alien in various ways that test your patience and challenge your imagination, he's still a person, a unique, individual human being, which brings us to the next important point:

Fact Number 3: HE IS WHO HE IS. It's a safe bet that your partner probably isn't going to change dramatically no matter how much couples counseling you get, no matter how many relationship seminars you attend, no matter how many self-help books you shove in his face, no matter how many "Honey, we need to talk" conversations you initiate, no matter how many times you threaten to leave unless he gets with the program. People typically make small, significant changes, but their essential nature doesn't change that much, especially those who are in their thirties, forties, and beyond.

For example, it may drive you crazy that your partner drags his feet and is chronically late, since you place a high value on promptness. You may try various behavioral strategies, such as setting the clock ahead, reminding him to hurry, or giving him fifteen minutes' leeway so that you don't end up pacing at the front door getting angrier and angrier as your blood pressure soars. You can adapt in any number of ways, any or all of which may yield some marked improvement, but it's unrealistic to expect your partner to have a personality change and suddenly be ready fifteen minutes ahead of schedule. He is who he is, and while he may make small changes in the right direction, it's highly unlikely that he'll ever be ready before you are.

It's also important not to misinterpret your partner's essential nature as a reflection of his love and commitment. For example, let's say your mate resists having meaningful conversations or has trouble revealing his innermost feelings. He withdraws, you take it personally (I've yet to meet a woman who doesn't!), although he insists his behavior has nothing to do with you. He's probably telling the truth, but that doesn't necessarily reassure you, nor does it solve the problem of wanting a deeper emotional connection with your mate. So what would help? Behavioral strategies—timing, communication techniques, and other concrete measures—can help both of you to resolve fundamental differences.

What doesn't help is to keep repeating the same approach when it isn't making a tangible difference in your relationship. I'm reminded of the AA (Alcoholics Anonymous) definition of *insanity*: doing the same thing over and over and expecting a different result. I'm struck by the lengths women go to when trying to alter their partner's behavior by trying to get him to change, despite his ongoing resistance (not to mention the frustration and emotional drain that comes with beating our heads against a wall).

This brings up a conversation I've been having with my mom for the past twenty years. She has often accused couples my age of being cavalier and not committed to their relationships, saying, "As soon as something goes wrong, they're out the door." I've long taken offense at the criticism that our generation isn't serious about commitments and that we blithely file for divorce when things get difficult, especially given the degree of agony and soul-searching that accompanied my divorces.

But I'm starting to think my mom is right, at least in this way: Whereas married couples of our parents' and grandparents' generation stayed together (not always for the right reasons), they did seem to be more skilled at accepting their spouses' imperfections and idiosyncrasies rather than seeking to change their partner or prematurely filing for divorce. I remember Grandma Sophie putting up with Papa Philip's somewhat overbearing personality and just shrugging, smiling, and saying, usually affectionately, "Oh, that's Philip," as if to imply that obviously, we all have annoying habits or personality traits that simply come with the territory.

Flash-forward: My parents constantly squabble about the most trivial things, such as, why didn't she pour him a full cup of coffee? Is the restaurant on the right or the left side of the street? Their bickering drives me up the wall, but it doesn't seem to bother them in the slightest. They're about to celebrate their fiftieth anniversary, so they must be doing something right.

Unquestionably, there are couples who are better off apart, both for themselves and for their children. And I still believe that for most of us, the decision to divorce is painful and heart wrenching, something we don't take lightly. But maybe we need to lighten up a bit on our intense belief that if we just keep at it, we can get our partner to change in order to meet our expectations.

In my book *Loving an Imperfect Man* I pose the question: Do women have unrealistic expectations of men? My answer continues to be an emphatic *No!* However, we may be sabotaging ourselves by overwhelming our partner in one of two ways: by confronting him with too many issues at once, or by communicating our feelings in a manner that increases his resistance and pushes him away.

Case in point: In my workshops, when I ask women to make a list of what is missing or what they want from their partners, they typically come up with at least a dozen ways in which they wish he would change (improve). When I ask men the same question here's how they typically respond: "I wish she would leave me alone."

Now, before you say, "He wants me to leave him alone? Fine. I'll leave him alone. I'll leave him alone for good," consider the subtext. When men say they want to be left alone, they're really saying, "I want her to accept me as I am." Of course, they may also be saying, "I don't want to look at myself," or "I don't want to look at our relationship," or "I don't want to deal with tough issues that may force me to have to confront my fears or face my limitations."

Throughout this book you will learn numerous useful strategies to disarm your partner's fears and resistance. But for now it's important to remember that at the heart of his resistance lies a deep longing for unconditional love. Deep down, that's what we all want. It's the single most difficult thing to do, and the one thing that will truly make a difference in our relationships.

At this point you may be asking, "But isn't it a two-way

street?" In other words, why should you keep knocking yourself out trying anything and everything to improve your relationship while your partner either denies any problems or resents your efforts?

The answer is simple: because you want to be sure you've given this relationship your best shot; and because you have nothing to lose and everything to gain by approaching your relationship in a new way.

Remember: No one is forcing you to be in this relationship. There are reasons why you chose and are continuing to choose the primary man in your life, which brings us to Fact Number 4.

Fact Number 4: YOU HAVE CHOICES. We may feel stuck in our relationship, but we have far more power than we think. We aren't victims. We have choices regarding every single issue that bothers us in our relationship. One, of course, is to leave the relationship, but that's the last resort. There's a whole lot we can do before getting to that point.

For instance, consider the man mentioned earlier in this introduction whose wife is upset at how emotionally unavailable he is. She can complain till the cows come home. Or she can try a variety of perfectly good options: She can ask her husband to at least sit down and listen to her feelings, even if he's unwilling to reveal his own. She can share some of her feelings with her friends or a therapist. She can alter her expectations, which doesn't mean that she has to like her husband's lack of emotional response, and neither does it mean giving lip service by saying it's "okay" while secretly resenting him. *Altering expectations doesn't mean settling.* Rather, it means choosing a more realistic approach to having all that's possible with this particular human being. In short, if you want to create real and lasting change in your relationship, you have to be willing to try some new and different strategies.

The primary strategy presented throughout this book—and perhaps its most radical message—is to DO WHAT WORKS! Without resorting to the "Rules"—without in any way encouraging you to be coy, manipulative, or compromising about your integrity—I urge you to start approaching your partner in a smarter, more strategic way. For example, if waiting to talk to your mate until he's in bed works, then wait! If wearing sexy lingerie works, then do it! If writing a thank-you note when he takes on more responsibility around the house or with the kids works—then by all means, get out your stationery. If being a bit more reserved, independent, or mysterious works, then give it a try! Worrying about doing the right thing isn't getting women anywhere, so this is a wake-up call. Consider this a postfeminist, post–politically correct book. What we want is to make substantial changes, which means using everything at our disposal.

To repeat: *You have more power than you think.* There are simple solutions to every single problem experienced in intimate relationships with men *if* we're willing to be creative in our approach. This book gives you practical, doable solutions that *will* work. Each chapter includes an overview of the issues, a short explanation (not excuse) for his behavior, our part of the puzzle, what emotionally hooks us, and most importantly, concrete suggestions for solving the problem. By the time you finish this book, you will be much clearer about the man you're involved with, what is and isn't possible, and how to enhance what you have, all of which is about making *your* life and your relationship smoother, happier, and infinitely more fulfilling.

1

If he doesn't understand why you're reading this book (or "get" all the ways in which you try to strengthen your relationship)

———◆———

W ho cares? Okay, maybe you do care. Let's be honest; most of us wish our partner would acknowledge and appreciate our considerable efforts to improve the quality of our relationship. Wouldn't it be nice, for example, if your partner noticed that you're reading this book and did any or all of the following:

- ask why
- leaf through it
- leaf through it and comment on specific issues that apply to him
- borrow it to read when you're finished
- or, best of all, suggest that you read it together and talk about everything in it that relates to the two of you

It's a lovely fantasy. But it probably won't materialize. Granted, it would be terrific if your partner was intrigued by and engaged in your ongoing efforts to improve your communication, deepen your intimacy, and handle thorny issues that arise. Unfortunately that's asking a lot. It's not because men are illiterate or insensitive. And it's not because they don't care, although at times it may feel that way. Contrary to what we may think, our partner's response to our overt attempts at enhancing intimacy isn't a reflection of his commitment or his love.

So why do we continue to feel disappointed when our partner doesn't place the same value as we do on improving our relationship? In part because we tend to place symbolic value on our partner's behavior when, in reality, his response has little or nothing to do with us.

Imagine, for example, that you're interested in signing up for a weekend relationship seminar offered by your church or synagogue. You're willing to set aside the time and invest the money; you've even thought of inviting your closest friends, Bill and Sandy, to join you. You bring up the idea over dinner, excited at the prospect of spending a weekend "working" on your relationship, although you're prepared for him to need a little coaxing. You explain the details and wait expectantly for his response. He fidgets with his food, mumbles something about golf, walks into the living room, and turns on the TV. You follow him, insisting that he give you one good reason why you shouldn't attend the seminar. "Can we talk about it later?" he asks. No. It's Wednesday and you need an answer. You get an answer. Looking more than mildly irritated, he says, "Our relationship is fine. Why would I want to spend my weekend sitting in a room with a bunch of strangers whining about problems we don't even have when I could be out on the golf course with my friends?" (Thank God you never mentioned Bill and Sandy or he'd really freak out!) You stomp out of the room, furious that your partner cares more about hitting a little ball into a hole than saving your marriage, which must be in even worse shape than you thought.

Or let's say you try to read a portion of this book out loud to your partner. A certain passage strikes you as being extremely relevant to issues in your relationship. You start reading and your mate interrupts midsentence to ask when the carpet cleaners are coming. You slam the book shut and tell him to "Forget it. Obviously you couldn't care less about what's in this book."

Bingo! You're right. He may not care about hearing the content of this book or talking about other relationship-related issues. But that doesn't mean that he doesn't care about you. (Remember: The rule is to reverse a double negative; in other words, he does care about you even if he doesn't share your interest in self-help books, couples counseling, relationship seminars, or other means of improving intimacy.)

There is, however, a difference between being disinterested and being dismissive or downright rude. The point is that you're reading this book—or making other efforts to improve your relationship—because doing so feels right and worthwhile to you. That's all you need to be concerned with, unless your mate ridicules or makes disparaging remarks about what you're doing, in which case, stand up for yourself and don't let his attitude undermine your enthusiasm.

Do what you do for yourself. Using the metaphor of this book, your mate doesn't have to read it, like it, or like the fact that you're reading it. Actually, the most likely scenarios are: Either he'll skim through it, laugh, and say something relatively benign and somewhat endearing such as, "Fifteen, huh? So what's my score?" (Why do they have to make sports metaphors out of everything?) Or he'll snort sarcastically and say something like, "I see you're wasting more good money on another one of those stupid chick books," which actually means, "Oh, oh. I wonder if I'm in worse trouble than I thought." In other words, he may be threatened, which leads us to the following question.

WHY ARE THEY LIKE THIS?

Just to reassure you that you're not alone, relatively few men read self-help books, and even fewer initiate "feelings conversations," couples counseling, or relationship seminars. (Yes, thousands of men attend John Gray's *Men Are from Mars, Women Are from Venus* workshops. Although it doesn't take a rocket scientist to predict this statistic, I'd bet my mortgage that at least twice as many women as men are the ones who sign up for the seminar—and that's probably being conservative.)

Why is this? First and foremost, men in general are loath to accept advice, unless it's from their stockbroker, car mechanic, or boss, and only then because they don't have a choice. Whereas most women are open to input, men avoid advice like the plague, which, in fact, is a fairly good analogy, in that to men taking advice implies acknowledging that they need help (that they're incompetent, confused, or ailing), which is a matter of swallowing pride, something men choke on, even when they'd benefit from the input.

Along the same lines, reading a self-help book or attending a relationship seminar is tantamount to admitting that they have a "problem," which most men would just as soon ignore or avoid. (If we don't talk about it, maybe it will just go away.)

Now, of course, *we* know that exploring relationship issues is a sign of health, a positive step toward strengthening ourselves and our partnership. But men don't know that. Instead they assume that self-help books, counseling, and other therapeutic endeavors are for "people with problems" rather than individuals who are healthy enough to pursue a deeper, more enduring connection.

That's just how men are. (Again, there are exceptions to every rule.) Stop and think: How many times have you brought up a difficult issue to your partner only to be accused of "causing" the problem by having mentioned it in the first place? I'm working on a name for this one. It's a version of "shoot the messenger": First we struggle to figure out the best way to bring up the issue (without provoking an argument or putting our partner on the defensive); then we summon the guts to initiate a conversation about "difficult stuff"; and then we end up being reproached for delivering the information. No wonder we're stumped. If we don't bring the issue up, nothing changes. If we do, we run the risk of a conflict. That doesn't leave us with any good option. (Not to fear: see Simple Solutions about this in chapter 12). For now, suffice it to say that seeking relationship help falls into a category we might call: "I'd rather eat nails than sit around thinking about or talking to strangers about my personal problems, much less paying good money to do so."

My second husband, Joey, fell into this category. Early in our relationship the subject of marital therapy came up.

Joey jokingly said, "If our relationship ever gets so bad that you want us to go to therapy, I'll just pin a note on you saying, 'Fix her and send her back when she can live with me and love me the way I am.' " At the time I found his comment witty and adorable. Three years later, when the blush was gone from our romance, I discovered he'd meant this quite literally. Sure enough, I had to drag him to our one and only therapy session; eventually we divorced, in part because of his refusal to deal with our issues in this particular way, and partly because of my stubborn insistence that this was the only way to do so.

Finally, it's important to know that your partner's lack of overt interest in sharing this book or other efforts at building intimacy doesn't necessarily indicate that he's oblivious to your feelings or to the issues in your relationship. He'd simply rather not read about or talk about these issues, and seeing, for example, you reading this book (and probably discussing it with your friends) may make him feel vulnerable and exposed.

The more threatened your partner feels, the more likely he is to act out by being disrespectful toward you. If, for example, he reacts by ridiculing you (saying you're a "self-help junkie"—so what; you could have worse addictions), by confronting you (saying, "I suppose you're going to read that book and then go off about all the things that are wrong with me"), or, worst of all, shaming you (saying, "If you were as smart as you think you are you wouldn't keep going to so-called experts for advice") it may be because he's terrified of what you might discover about yourself and your relationship. Remember: *Knowledge is power.* Your partner's insecurities will surface if he feels threatened that you may be thinking seriously about what needs changing in your relationship, or it may evoke his worst fear, although he'd never admit it, that you'll end up realizing he's not Mr. Right and you deserve better.

There are ways to reassure your partner, which we'll get to in a moment, but for now it's essential to know that *you needn't explain yourself, defend yourself, or even reveal that you're reading this book or pursuing other ways to improve your relationship.*

But first: Read the following very carefully. To prevent any potential misunderstanding, I'm not suggesting that you hide this book from your partner or keep it a secret. In their best-selling book *The Rules*, coauthors Ellen Fein and Sherrie Schneider urge readers not to let their partner, friends, or therapist know that they're reading it, which is both appalling and frightening. It's censorship at its worst—withholding important information for fear of disapproval or criticism. Any book, seminar, or other means of gaining relationship advice should be strong enough to hold up to scrutiny, challenge, and intelligent debate. There is a difference, for example, between hiding this book from your partner and consciously choosing how, when, and why you choose to share it, or perhaps choosing not to share it at all.

Here's how to decide: If you trust your partner to be supportive, or at least neutral in his response, then by all means, show it, read passages aloud, keep it on your nightstand, do whatever feels right. If your mate acts a little put off, then you make the call. You're a big girl; you can handle a little questioning, jabbing, or even criticism, if it's all in good fun or fodder for stimulating conversation.

If, on the other hand, based on experience you anticipate that your partner will be disdainful or even abusive, then why give him the opportunity to hurt you? There's no rule that says you have to share everything. After all, you probably don't show him every article you read in *Mirabella* or every camisole you admire in the Victoria's Secret catalog. Some things are meant for you alone, and if your mate can't be supportive of your reading this or any other self-help books, joining a women's support group, or attending a workshop, then don't give him any ammunition. Frankly, it's his loss. Ironically, despite his fears, everything in this book, for instance, is designed to increase your acceptance and appreciation of your mate and to give you strategies for improving your relationship. Regardless of his reaction, he will reap the benefits. But don't waste your breath reading him the previous sentence. It's tempting to invoke an "expert's" words to persuade our partner of our point of view, but this is just another way of putting your energy into changing him instead of staying focused on yourself. Instead, keep reading as we go on to explore how we, as women, may unknowingly undermine our own success by the way we respond to our partner's lack of reciprocity in pursuing deeper intimacy.

HOW WE MAKE IT WORSE

Whether or not we like it, we have a part in each and every dynamic in our relationship. What we feel, say, and do has a significant impact on our partner's behavior, and vice versa, in what is often referred to as the "dance" of relationships.

In other words, it takes two to tango. We aren't flawless, no one is, and even if we believe that our partner has a bigger part in creating the issues in our relationship, we still have to take responsibility for how we react, play into, or even provoke his behavior.

Regarding the issue at hand, the biggest error women make is in pushing or manipulating our partner to express interest in or participate in what we care about, regardless of his feelings. For instance, we may shove this book in his face, insisting he read it, or read passages aloud, forcing him to be a captive audience, emphasis on the word *captive*. We may taunt him by making sarcastic, biting, or loaded comments based on the material and use it to get his goat. We may get angry at his lack of interest and start a fight, accusing him of being clueless or an ostrich, sticking his head in the sand rather than being willing to honestly look at issues in our relationship. We may act out by using the book as a subtle threat, reminding him that he's up to Number Eight, so he'd better listen up or else . . ."

All of the above responses to his lack of interest are understandable, but they just plain won't work. We want our partner to "get it," and we think we can help him "get it" by involving him in reading this book, exploring his feelings, or sharing other ways in which we are trying to improve our relationship. But instead of his "getting it," he's only going to get mad when we impose our agenda and pressure him when he either couldn't care less, has better things to do, or for all the reasons discussed earlier, would rather not delve into this material.

Another way in which we contribute to the problem is by making *our* way the *right* way instead of respecting the fact that our mate has a different way of dealing with his feelings. Just because we find it useful to actively pursue personal growth and the strengthening of our relationship doesn't mean that our way is the only or the best way to gain insight or explore meaningful issues. Our partner may think about the same things while he's trimming the hedges or working on his car; he may even talk about them with some of his friends. When we're self-righteous, using ourselves as the standard of excellence against which we judge his way of doing things, we are being disrespectful and driving more of a wedge between ourselves and our mate.

It's hard to stop. Why? *Because we care so much.* Besides, we're pretty sure we're on the right track and that if he'd only just be receptive to what we have to share, our relationship would be in a lot better shape. Maybe so, maybe not. Pressuring our partner is rarely effective, and then, only when our partner is up against the wall, willing to do anything to salvage the marriage and regain our goodwill. Hopefully, your relationship isn't in these dire straits, in which case it's much more effective to back off and let your mate explore his feelings in his own way rather than imposing on him your own agenda or criticizing him for being who he is.

Our intense feelings are what make this so challenging. We want so badly for our partner to be an active participant in our pursuits that even when we promise ourselves to leave him alone, even when we make a pact with our best friend that we'll stop nudging him or resenting his lack of involvement, we may have trouble keeping our commitment. That's because of how hurt, angry, and disappointed we may feel, which is one of the reasons you're reading this book, and one of the reasons you may wish he would do the same.

WHAT HOOKS US

Ideally, we would be able to blow off (accept, understand, let go of) the things our partner does or doesn't do that make us frustrated or angry. But that's easier said than done. It's hard to detach and keep saying "it's okay" when it really doesn't feel okay. Even when we're able to say to ourselves "no big deal" or "that's just the way he is," we may be seething inside.

We're *human,* which means we get angry, bummed out, and just plain hurt. In short, we get emotionally hooked. Throughout this book we'll explore the "emotional hooks"—what really bothers us about the specific issue we're talking about.

In this case, the emotional aspect is related to our investment in our relationship and our anger that our mate may not be equally invested. Every hour we spend thinking about how to solve a problem in our relationship, every conversation we have with friends about the best way to approach our partner, every single dollar we spend on yet another self-help book, seminar, or counseling session represents the magnitude of our commitment to our mate and to our relationship. Meanwhile, we keep hoping he'll meet us halfway, or at least take some steps in the right direction.

We're simply getting sick of doing all, or most of, the investing. Granted, we are *choosing* to do so; no one held you at gunpoint, said, "Hand over the money, lady," and forced you to buy and read this book. But somehow that doesn't matter. The more we invest—and the less our mate reciprocates—the angrier we get. Each time our partner assures us he's willing to try and then capitulates, we get emotionally hooked—maybe *this* time he'll come through!

Nancy, a woman in one of my workshops, says, "I've been in a women's support group for eight years. I've worked really hard at looking at my issues, and I still can't get my husband, Brad, to spend more than twenty minutes talking about what's going on in our relationship. Here's what I told Nancy: Give it up. Instead of trying to "get" Brad to change, simply do what you want and learn what you can, whether or not Brad is open or willing to participate.

When we are the one doing all the "relationship mainte-nance" and especially if we're getting criticized for doing so, we're bound to feel that something isn't fair. It isn't. But, as I will repeatedly stress throughout this book, the smartest approach to solving relationship problems with men is to forget about what's "fair" and think about what "works." To do so, start with the following simple solutions.

SIMPLE SOLUTIONS

If you want your mate to be more involved in relationship building, MAKE IT A CHOICE rather than an ultimatum or demand. Giving our partner a choice has two distinct re-wards. First, he doesn't feel pressured and therefore he has no reason to be on the defensive. If it's *his* choice, he can say yes, no, maybe, or later, but it's his decision and it isn't going to turn into a power struggle, which is what he wants to avoid at all costs. Second, giving him a choice puts us in a much better position. We offer to share some-thing that's important to us, but we don't go so far out on a limb as to risk criticism or other negative repercussions.

Be careful, however, that you're giving him a "clean" choice, in other words, that there's no strings attached. The only way to protect yourself and increase the possibil-ity of his responding in a positive way is to GIVE HIM THE CHOICE WITHOUT A VESTED INTEREST IN THE OUTCOME. This sounds easy, but it requires being quite self-aware. We're not always conscious of how emotionally invested we are in our mate's coming through for us. For example, if you mention that it's been weeks since the two of you have really had time to sit down and talk about how your relationship is going and he says, "You know, I was thinking we should go away this weekend to a cabin and spend some quiet time just being together" (I know. Where is this man?), it's tempting to throw a party and invite the world. If, on the other hand, he says, "Here we go again. I knew we couldn't just have fun together without having to talk about our feelings," it's natural to feel embarrassed or put off. But you haven't done anything wrong. He's simply not ready or willing to be emotionally present, in which case, it's time to back off. And what to do about *your* feelings? Call a friend. Take a walk. Write in your journal and keep repeating to yourself: I feel good about doing everything I can to improve our relationship.

The second simple solution is to ONLY SHARE ASPECTS OF YOUR SEARCH FOR RELATIONSHIP ANSWERS THAT YOU FEEL ARE ESPECIALLY RELEVENT AND POTENTIALLY HELPFUL TO YOUR RELATIONSHIP. It's normal to get excited when we read or hear something that rings true, especially if it reinforces our point of view and confirms our "take" on our relationship. Again, proceed with caution. Remember: This is about being smart, safe, and strategic. For example, you may choose to share part of a therapy appointment that was particularly powerful and/or relates to your relationship, but you needn't feel compelled to give your partner every detail of the session. Or if you choose to read or point out a certain passage in this book, be careful to do so in a way that doesn't alienate or offend him. For instance, even if you've been fighting for years over his being a "weekend dad" instead of an equal parent, resist the urge to highlight the section on how men should do their share. Don't lean over his shoulder while he's reading or say, "See, I'm not the only one who feels this way!" Don't gloat. Don't push it. Don't use this book as an object lesson because it will blow up in your face. The instant your mate feels the slightest pressure, he's likely to put the book down, if not hurl it across the room with a few chosen expletives to make his point. If you choose to share some of the content, do so in a spirit of love and camaraderie. And it doesn't hurt to say, "Thanks for reading that" or "It really helped to talk to you about my therapy session." This may seem like pandering, but appreciation goes a long way, and, besides, what does it cost you to go the extra mile?

Whether you choose to share this book or keep it off-limits, there certainly are others—close friends, for example—with whom you could share your experience. GO TO WHERE YOU CAN COUNT ON RECEIVING ENCOURAGEMENT AND SUPPORT. Think about it. Which would you rather do? Read your mate a passage of this book that's likely to provoke a scene or read the same passage to your best friend who giggles, sighs, and tells you the wonderfully gory details of the latest episode with her mate? In other words, learn how to go to a full well. What matters is for you to share only your personal feelings and discoveries with those individuals who "get it," who take you seriously and respect your efforts to improve yourself and your relationship. And regardless of whether or not you can share your process with others, give yourself credit for your continuing efforts to grow and to help your relationship grow.

ON THE BRIGHT SIDE

Whatever you do, whether you decide to share some, all, or none of what you're learning with your partner, it's your choice! There's something to be said for protecting (and savoring) your private life. For example, it may be much more fun to keep this book off-limits from your mate. The bonus: Your partner may get curious, intrigued, and even a little paranoid about what you're reading, which may lead to his asking—even begging—you to let him in on the secret. Wait.

Enjoy this moment and keep reading.

2

If he doesn't do his share

Next on the list is one of the most universal complaints: He doesn't help out enough. As one woman put it: "There's a pile of dirty dishes in the sink, the hamper's overflowing, one kid's crying, the other needs help with homework, the whole family's coming over tomorrow morning for his mother's birthday, I have an urgent work deadline, and I'm running around ready to drop, while he's sitting in front of the TV saying, 'Honey, relax. Everything will be okay.' "

What's the deal? Do men have a selfish gene or are they actually that oblivious to what's going on around them? In your wildest imagination could you ever picture yourself stretched out with a magazine when the hamper's overflowing, the kids are starving, or the phone's ringing off the hook? We will visit and revisit this particular dilemma throughout this book, since the issue of men not giving as much as women comes up in a variety of areas, whether it's about housework, parenting, buying family birthday gifts, or initiating emotional intimacy.

Granted, there's something to be said for being laid-back, for not being type A and perfectionists about everything getting done right this minute in exactly the right way. In all fairness, there are plenty of men who do their fair share of work around the house. My father happens to be one of them. Bob, my best friend Jill's husband, is another. When I'm invited to dinner, he literally vacuums between courses. But they're the exceptions. If you're one of the lucky ones whose partner does his share (especially without being constantly reminded and rewarded), thank your lucky stars and turn the page.

Bet you're still reading. In general, even the most giving men seem to slack off when it comes to taking responsibility for their full 50 percent. Yes, most men work hard, but so do most women, whether we're in the workforce, caring for children, or juggling a combination of both. Yet we still manage to give an enormous amount, which makes us ask the following question.

WHY ARE THEY LIKE THIS?

Without excavating the male psyche, it's worthwhile to take a moment to look at a few of the reasons why men, in general, fail to do their fair share. Saying that they're just plain born or bred to be selfish is a little too easy, although there's some real truth to this argument. Actually, a blend of genetics and upbringing are the culprits in this case.

My friend Louis and I have argued this one so many

times that he's finally convinced me to at least consider the possibility that men aren't selfish, they're simply not meant to be making beds, bathing babies, or serving dinner. He loves to present the "caveman" argument, which goes something like: "Contemporary relationships don't work because women expect men to go against their nature." He insists that relationships worked best back in the good old days, when men went out hunting and fishing while women sat around the fire, preparing the kill and keeping the cave lights burning. Fair enough. Meanwhile, I'm still looking for a man who will make a fabulous living so that I can stay home raising babies and baking brownies, but they appear to be few and far between.

His point, however, is well taken. Perhaps men and women are primarily wired to naturally assume different responsibilities, which may account for why men don't do their share, given that what we need is for them to go to the office and stop on the way home to take money out of the ATM machine, buy some frozen hamburgers, and pitch in around the house, which, by the way, requires two incomes to support in 90 percent of families.

Also, there's no question that as a result of their upbringing the majority of men believe that women are responsible for taking care of most everything, including them. Although many contemporary men are actively involved in parenting, most men of the baby boomer generation were primarily cared for by their mother, whom they watched do the lion's share of child care and housework, often working outside the home, whether professionally or on a volunteer basis, while their father relaxed after coming home from a hard day's work (as if taking care of kids, home, community, etc., isn't work!).

Nevertheless, the message was: Dad makes a living, and

Mom does everything else (in some cases, including making a living). Even though men have come a long way, and in many ways this anachronistic arrangement no longer applies, this image remains firmly embedded in men's brains.

But understanding the underlying reasons for men's behavior doesn't *excuse* them; it simply helps *explain* why they are the way they are, which is useful in terms of helping us to understand their behavior a little better. What matters more is to see how men's makeup and conditioning is manifested in our present relationship, right here, right now.

If you need hard numbers to convince you that, on balance, you probably do more than your partner does, check this out. A few years ago the book *The Second Shift*, described the ongoing phenomenon of women working all day at a career and then coming home and putting in an inequitable number of hours doing everything else required to keep a home and a family running smoothly. The author, Arlie Hochschild, offers a dramatic statistic: According to her research, when you add it up, the average woman puts in a full month's more work hours per year than the average man. She defines "work" as covering everything that takes time and energy, including career, carpooling, grocery shopping, making dinner, washing dishes, taking care of kids, making social plans, maintaining family ties, not to mention being the source of most of the emotional comfort in your intimate relationship. If this statistic is confusing, here's an easy interpretation: If you compare how much you do to how much your partner does, it's the same as if he took a full month's vacation every year.

So what's the solution? Does being in an intimate relationship with a man mean being eternally doomed to doing more than your share? Absolutely not! I will show you how to improve the situation, but first let's take a look at our own part in having created the problem.

HOW WE MAKE IT WORSE

When it comes to doing more than our share, we may have set up a pattern early in our relationship in which we inadvertently excused our partner's lack of participation and compensated by picking up the slack. There are several reasons why this happens. For starters, most women have been raised to believe that it's up to us to make everything okay and to give and give and give, even when doing so is draining and exhausting.

We also may hesitate to pressure our partner and instead do his share so as to avoid a confrontation. (Or, as women in my Indispensable Women workshops say: *It's easier to do it myself.*) And more often than not it *is* easier to do it ourselves than to have to keep asking, pushing, reminding, and explaining what needs to be done. In any or all of these ways, we've had a part in creating the pattern, which we must now carefully undo.

Changing a pattern may seem difficult, perhaps even more trouble than it's worth, but it's not. It just takes altering our behavior and having the patience to give our partner time to improve. But in order to do so, we have to understand which of our emotional buttons are being pushed when our partner fails to do his share.

WHAT HOOKS US

Why do we get so bent out of shape when our partner doesn't do his share?

It's pretty simple. What really ticks us off is that it's *just not fair!* The injustice makes us feel like screaming: What about *me?* Why do I have to do all the work without nearly enough acknowledgment and appreciation? It's even more infuriating when our partner doesn't acknowledge how overwhelmed and stressed-out we are from managing the countless competing demands in our lives.

It's *not* fair. Partly it's a matter of principle, partly it's infuriating because having to do so much is physically exhausting and makes us resent our partner. Now anyone with half a brain knows that we shouldn't have to jump through hoops to get him to empty the dishwasher or notice that we're running out of milk and stop at the store on his way home without E-mailing him at work. But guess what? That may be exactly what it takes—and this book is about doing what it takes to get what we want. So forget the "shoulds." Yes, he should do his share. It's his house, his kids, his family, his friends, so there's no good reason on earth why he should have to be asked instead of naturally doing what's needed. But *should*s are useless here, as I will repeatedly say throughout this book. What he should do is irrelevant. What *you* can do and what choices you can make to get more of what you want are the only things that enable change to occur and alter how you feel in your relationship.

Knowing your choices and acting on them is what makes the difference between resentment and acceptance. Remember: Your goal is to diminish your frustration and increase your satisfaction. With this in mind, here are some ways to approach your partner in a way that will maximize success.

SIMPLE SOLUTIONS

First, ASK NICELY FOR WHAT YOU WANT. Admit it, what you (and all of us) really want is for your partner to read your mind and just naturally do his share. Here's the fantasy: He knows you've had a hell week at work, the house is a mess, you're on the verge of getting your period, and you're so bloated you don't have anything to wear out to dinner tonight. He tucks you in for a nap, and when you awake, the entire house is clean. He drives you to the mall and finds you the perfect outfit to wear. You go to the restaurant relaxed, rested, and looking like a million dollars. If this describes the man you love, let's clone him, because, believe me, he's a prince. But that just isn't how it works with most men. Even when they're willing to do a little more, they still need directions that are carefully spelled out in a way they can accept without becoming defensive.

In others words, we have to ask for what we want. And we have to ask in a courteous way. No matter how angry we may be (it's easy to explode when you're sitting on years of accumulated anger), screaming, threatening, and shaming don't get us the response we desire.

So just accept the fact that you will have to ask for what you want, and if you are serious about getting results, you'll have to be strategic in your approach. First, here's what *not* to do: Resist the temptation to tell him he's a lazy no-good slob who doesn't lift a finger to help. (For one thing, this probably isn't true. Unless he's a total loser, he is doing something; whether or not it's enough we'll get to in a minute.) Also, resist the urge to exaggerate in order to get your point across. Saying "You never help with the kids" or "I do every single thing around here while you sit on your butt" is overstating your case and is sure to enrage and antagonize him.

So what's the right approach? Try saying "Please fold the laundry" or "I'd really appreciate it if you'd help Jeff study for his test." I know it's annoying to have to choose your words carefully; doing so may seem like coddling your partner, but keep your end goal in sight: The whole idea is to get him to do more, and your best chance of success is to keep it simple and express your desires in the form of a request.

Next, Be Specific. Men respond far better to concrete requests than to vague threats or emotional outbursts. Saying "If you don't start helping out around here, I'll . . ." isn't useful. Neither is "You have to take on more responsibility or I'm going to crack." You may feel this way—don't we all?—but, remember, we're trying to change patterns here, and that means approaching your partner in a new way, in this case asking nicely, being specific, and being careful not to overwhelm him with too many requests at once.

Start by figuring out one or two ways in which you want your partner to take on more of his share. For example, it might be, "From now on I'd like you to be in charge of dinner twice a week" or "I want you to start driving the Sunday school car pool beginning this Sunday." He may say yes, he may say no. He may say sure, and then act as if the conversation never happened, which we'll explore in chapter 13, which is about breaking promises. (This is another one of the "Biggies"—he says he'll do something and he either pretends it never happened, does it for a while and then regresses, or does it grudgingly so that *you* end up looking like the bad guy.)

Of course, when you ask your partner to do something,

you have to be prepared for the possibility of his saying no, which is where NEGOTIATION enters into the picture.

The idea of negotiating may not sound romantic or fit into your concept of an intimate relationship, but it's a tactic that men respond to. Remember: The goal is to *do what works.* In this case your objective is to negotiate a more equitable division of labor. The smoothest relationships are ones in which each partner does what he or she does best, gives what he or she gives most naturally, with hopefully it all balancing out in the end. The best way to negotiate an equitable division of labor is to sit down with your partner and write down every single task that's involved in running your lives and your household. Then put a check mark next to who actually does what. Seeing everything written down in black and white removes some of the emotional intensity and forces each of you to really see what the other is doing.

You might be surprised at how much your partner is contributing, you might feel vindicated by how much longer your list is than his, and you might disagree with each other about who's giving how much of what. If this turns into a debate or worse, a shouting match, stop immediately. Simply tape the list on the kitchen wall and agree that for the next two weeks each of you will check off everything you do. The whole point of doing this exercise is to define who is taking responsibility for what, so that you can use the list as a starting point for redistributing tasks.

To get the most out of this exercise, you need to LISTEN TO AND ACKNOWLEDGE YOUR MATE'S PERCEPTIONS OF WHAT HE DOES, whether or not you see it the way he does. For example, you might give him a grade of D– in the area of keeping an orderly home, but meanwhile he mows the lawn, does the taxes, changes the light bulbs, keeps your car in running order, and fixes the air conditioner when it breaks down. So as not to be sexist, it's just as possible that he does the majority of the child care or loves to cook but is a terrible procrastinator when it comes to raking leaves or balancing the checkbook. He may be doing all sorts of things that you're either unaware of or that don't count for you because of how angry you are about all the things he's not doing.

What's equitable is entirely subjective, depending on what works for you and your partner. Every couple makes agreements and contracts based on their unique needs. One couple may agree to share all housework and parenting responsibilities, while another may have worked out a deal in which one partner provides the majority of financial support while the other is responsible for most domestic tasks. All that matters is for you and your mate to agree on what's fair. Which brings us to the question of priorities.

One of the main reasons we end up doing more than he does is that we care more about certain things than he does. It doesn't bother *him* that your best friends are coming for dinner and there are cobwebs on the ceiling, but it bothers *you,* so you're on a chair with a broom . . . As far as *he's* concerned, it's just fine for the kids to have frozen pizza, but *you* insist that they have a healthy, balanced diet, which means you're making broccoli casserole while he's reading *Sports Illustrated.* Here's how the formula works: Whatever matters to you that doesn't matter to him ends up on your list, which is one of the reasons you end up doing more than your share.

So how do you either reconcile the inequity or find a compromise that works for you? The real trick is to GIVE

ONLY AS MUCH AS YOU GENUINELY WANT TO GIVE. Don't compare what you give to what he gives, don't be a martyr, and don't be an Indispensable Woman, wearing yourself out to make a point. Sure it's incredibly maddening when we do most of the work. Even more so when our partner not only doesn't participate, but also ignores our effort or gives us grief, adding insult to injury.

Take the following example. A few years ago when I was married to Joey, his sister Martha and I decided to throw a surprise sixtieth birthday party for his mother at our house. Now, understand: Joey had zero obligations. Martha and I planned the party, sent the invitations, made the food, and cleaned up after. Joey never offered to help. In fact, all he did was whine about what a mess there would be and why did I have to go to all this trouble anyway? He wouldn't. His style would be to call his mom, wish her a happy birthday, and that would be that. But having the party was my choice. I didn't do it to get his approval or gain his mother's love. I did it because I enjoyed every minute of it, and that's the point. As long as we're doing what we want, we can give graciously and plentifully.

If you want your mate to do more, the worst thing you can do is pressure him. The slightest hint of a threat or ultimatum will automatically negate any willingness he has to negotiate, especially when it involves his signing up for more work and greater responsibility. The best results come when our partner feels free to choose. When it's his idea. When he gets to feel like a good guy instead of feeling resentful and pressured. As Nelson Mandela said, "Only free men can negotiate. Prisoners cannot enter into contracts."

Great words. Take them to heart.

Last but not least, have PATIENCE, MY DEAR! Changes take time, and we need to reward small, gradual changes, even if they're a far cry from our ultimate goal. Don't expect your partner's behavior to change overnight. Give it six months, a year, and then evaluate whether he's moving in the right direction. Any positive movement is an encouraging sign that change is possible.

ON THE BRIGHT SIDE

The most tangible perk, if you will, of having a partner who doesn't do his share is that when we do it all, we get to do it our way! This is the flip side of being an Indispensable Woman. Often women take on more than their share or allow their partner to do less than he should because they say, "It's easier to do it myself." In some cases, this is absolutely true. Obviously, it would be better for us if our mates helped out as much as we do. But if they don't, we can at least reap the benefits of having control over having an orderly home, appropriately dressed kids, getting necessary tasks completed, and all the other ways in which we've been waiting for him to come through. There is a real sense of power—and satisfaction—in a job well done, even if we have to do it ourselves.

3

If he says, "Stop acting like my mother!"

When men say "You're acting like my mother," what they really mean is:

- you're being pushy
- you're asking too many questions
- you're interfering in my business
- you're invading my privacy
- you must think I'm a moron
- you're making me feel like a child

Both as a woman and a mother, it's deeply disturbing that this is a man's worst insult and is meant to infuriate us and shake us up. More disturbingly, it works. That's why they keep doing it! When a man accuses his partner of being like his mother he is bringing out one of the most powerful weapons in his arsenal of ammunition—it is the "big gun" men pull out when they're especially uncomfortable, vulnerable, or don't know what else to say to recover their power and put us in our place. Personally, I find this "You're acting just like my mother" thing to be a particularly fascinating and unique part of the male psyche. Whether they love their mother, hate their mother, or feel something in between, their relationship with their mate is profoundly affected by the quality of their first intimate connection with a woman. Which is why, in meeting any prospective suitors, one of my first questions is: "Tell me about your relationship with your mother."

At least this behavior is somewhat predictable. It's hardly headline news that the quality of a man's relationship with his mother when he was young largely determines how he treats the woman he loves as an adult. But it's even more specific than that. For example, if a man felt smothered by his mother, he's likely to feel easily pressured by any unsolicited questions, suggestions, or advice on our part, regardless of how respectfully we pose them. If he felt criticized by his mother, even the slightest hint on our part that he's failing to meet our expectations gives rise to shame, which usually translates into his either withdrawing or going on the offensive.

For instance, we say, "Gee, honey, you really should go for that promotion," and he hears, "You've never been good enough, smart enough . . . Bam, he's back in grade school, feeling humiliated when he brought home his report card with the C+ in math and his mother berated him for being dumb. Or if his mother ignored or neglected him, he may both welcome and resent intimacy, which is a double whammy. If we get too close, he pulls back, having learned only to depend on himself, whereas if we aren't right there, he gets overly possessive, demanding, even irrationally jealous of what we're doing when we're not with him.

It's just plain insane. A good 75 percent of the time women feel as if they have to walk on eggshells, because our mere existence reminds him of his mother. We think he's responding to us, but for all intents and purposes, we may as well be wearing a mask with his mother's face on it, clad in her blue and white housedress, making meatloaf instead of sitting across from him in a restaurant in our favorite black dress thinking it's just the two of us. Wrong. There's three at the table, and one is invisible but ever present. Plus, being perceived as his "mother" denies our status as his lover and romantic partner.

How does this affect the normal workings in most relationships? In general, men project their "mother stuff" onto their mates by expressing feelings of being pressured. Although we certainly play our part in this exchange, and we definitely have ways of tempering our partner's response, we don't have any power over their unconscious projection of their "mother" feelings onto us. Before we explore our piece of the puzzle, let's take a moment to look at why men are so hung up on their mothers and act out accordingly.

WHY ARE THEY LIKE THIS?

Without getting into a complicated psychological analysis of Freud's famous Oedipus complex, suffice it to say that men are set up in their early adolescence to experience ambivalence, if not outright disdain, toward their mothers. The layman's explanation is that in order for boys to become men, they must separate (individuate is the psychological term) from the most primary and significant source of nurturing and love—their mom. According to Freud, a boy must actually reject his mother in order to succeed in this necessary passage into manhood.

The supposed inevitability of this has troubled me since the day my son, Evan, now a teenager, was born. As he has grown older, I've often wondered if this is inevitable, or if it has been historically unavoidable because of the fact that most boys are raised primarily, and in some cases solely, by their mothers. I figured I'd try a scientific experiment. Since Gary, Evan's father, has been equally present in his upbringing, I was eager to see whether Evan would experience a primal need to pull away from me in order to assert his manhood.

He did. And right on schedule, as if programmed by a genetic need to reject me, regardless of how involved his father was in his upbringing. I tried not to take it personally, but it hurt all the same. Two days before his bar mitzvah and his thirteenth birthday, my son, with whom I've had a very close, loving, and easygoing relationship, suddenly announced that he couldn't stand me. In fact, he couldn't stand anything about me. And oh, by the way, hadn't I noticed that whenever I called him at his dad's he was just being polite but couldn't wait to get off the phone? I was stunned. Evan's outburst hit me with the force of an unexpected blow to the head. I was shocked, horrified, and terrified that I'd finally and forever lost my sweet, sweet son. My heart was breaking, but I kept my composure and casually replied, "Welcome to being a teenager." Evan paced back and forth, insisting this had nothing to do with becoming a teenager, or maybe it had a little to do with it, he wasn't sure, but anyway, he couldn't stand me, and he just wanted that to be absolutely clear. It was past his bedtime, and an awkward moment ensued as Evan stood at my doorway, saying good night. It was the first time in nearly thirteen years he hadn't asked to be tucked in. "Good night," I replied casually. He shifted from foot to foot, there was a long pause, then my very precocious son came back into my room, sat down on my bed, and said, "Oh, I get what's going on. This is that thing where I stop wanting to marry you so that I can start liking girls, right?" "Right," I said, smiling, and then he let me tuck him into bed.

Based on my "scientific findings" I'm fairly well persuaded that this "I have to push Mom away in order to claim my manhood" thing is something real, and apparently somewhat inevitable regardless of how we raise our sons. This formula creates a difficult quandary both for men and for women, especially in intimate love relationships. Here's how it plays out. Boys' ambivalence and/or anger toward their mothers gets projected onto their mates in several ways. The boy needed his mother yet hated needing her, which translates into resenting women when we try to be there for men. The boy needed Mom's love yet felt her love exacted a huge price (his independence and autonomy), making him both long for and reject intimacy with women. The boy needed Mom's help yet felt he had to do it all on his own, which is why men tend to resist our efforts to be supportive, interpreting them as interference and pressure.

The operative word is *needed*. The boy's inability to reconcile his need for his mother translates directly into fear and confusion over needing his girlfriend, wife, or lover, which he experiences as pressure and deals with by saying, "Stop acting like my mother."

This is one area in which men get my genuine sympathy. Many men feel appropriately victimized (or to be less dramatic, negatively affected) by how they were treated by their mothers. And for good reason. Plenty of men had mothers who were either overbearing or overly needy, usually as a result of their own lack of fulfillment, either in their marriage or in other aspects of their lives. Mothers of men who are now in their forties or fifties may have depended on their identity as "mother" as their primary source of self-esteem. In many cases this resulted in mothers leaning too heavily on their sons for approval, companionship, and intimacy. Men in their twenties or thirties may have experienced a different but equally confusing dynamic as they watched their mothers struggle to gain independence and balance career and homemaking, often with overt resentment toward their husbands. I've listened to many, many men talk about how they felt they had to "take care" of their mother, which wasn't fair and often has a lasting effect on men's response to their intimate partner.

When I'm accused of acting like my partner's mother I'm tempted to say, "Get a grip! It's not 1965, you're not eleven, and I'm not your mother!" But here's the rub: Some of us *act* like we are our mate's mother, which leads us to the question of how we may unwittingly intensify this problem.

HOW WE MAKE IT WORSE

We, too, haven't fully escaped the effects of our upbringing. We've been deeply affected by our mother, our first and most significant role model, and may inadvertently take on her behavior not only with our children but also with our partners.

The biggest and most common mistake we make is in treating our partner like a child. I know, what are we supposed to do when he acts like a two-year-old? Hang on, the answer is coming. We may treat him like a child by telling him what to do, following around after him, making sure he does it, asking whether he's done it, and in many cases, doing it for him when he doesn't do it right.

This is the kiss of death. When we act like our partner's mother, we play right into his hands, pushing his "Mommy button" and giving him a justifiable reason to rebel. Regardless of whether we see him as immature and irresponsible, infantilizing him exacerbates the problem. He feels "little," which evokes shame and defensiveness, and we get nothing but aggravation out of the deal. It's a classic no-win situation that should be avoided at all costs.

Another way we act like our mate's mother is by being overbearing and invasive instead of respecting his boundaries. He naturally withdraws when we ask too many questions or insist that he continually answer to us. Lingering memories of his mother waiting up for him and asking for details about his date when she's the last person he wants to confide in make him recoil and want to run away. Even though we're just trying to be close, our partner experiences our interest as intrusion, which at its extreme, strips him of his manhood. When this occurs, expect him to react by pushing you away or saying hurtful things in order to recover his sense of power and individuality.

Third, being overly critical may restimulate negative feelings toward his mother, which he then transfers to us. For example, if your partner's mother was continually on his case, telling him to turn down the music, clean his room, get better grades, or choose more appropriate girlfriends, any criticism on your part gets all mixed up with his past pool of shame. The slightest recrimination, even gently reminding him to be home on time or asking why he still hasn't raked the leaves, gets filtered through his adolescent rage. The instant he hears (or thinks he hears) "You're not good enough," he immediately does one of two things: retreats or retaliates. He either goes away, literally or psychically, or he turns on you, with a barrage of criticism.

This may not seem fair—after all, we're just trying to help—but what *really* hurts us is how misunderstood we feel.

WHAT HOOKS US

The root of our emotional pain is that we genuinely believe that *we know what's best for our partner.* And we may be right. But our hands are tied because acting like his mother will always yield negative results. This puts us in a painful predicament. We love our mate and want to help him in any way we can. Just as it's painful to watch our children stumble over their feet and make what seems to be senseless mistakes, it's also hard to sit back and watch our partner blow it when we could easily intervene. This is especially frustrating when our mate's childish behavior directly affects our lives.

Randy, a woman in her late thirties who came to see me for counseling, shared her frustration with wanting to help her husband, Michael. She said, "Michael's been out of work for six months. Both of us are worried about money, and he's starting to get depressed. I've tried so hard to help him find a new job. I've helped him redo his résumé. I've started dozens of conversations about what he'd like to do, what he's good at, and what realistic possibilities exist in his field. I've cut out the Sunday classified ads, suggested he see a career counselor or headhunter, and the more I offer to help, the angrier he gets. Actually," Randy explains, "Michael's getting more passive. At first he was out there, making calls and going on interviews, but the longer this goes on, the more days he spends sitting in front of the television, feeling sorry for himself. I'm at my wit's end, but I can see that any help on my part is only making things worse."

Our sincere desire to help our partner be more of the man we want him to be can backfire when he takes our intentions the wrong way. So is there a right way to break the "Mom / little boy" pattern so that he can start acting like a grownup and we can stop feeling compelled to treat him like a child?

SIMPLE SOLUTIONS

Yes. Here's the trick: TREAT HIM LIKE AN ADULT. That's it. That's all there is to it. Now, here are four tangible ways to follow through:

First, STOP TELLING HIM WHAT TO DO OR HOW TO DO IT. This doesn't mean you have to sit on your hands and watch helplessly when he's about to screw up. There are numerous ways to offer feedback without coming across as being superior or patronizing. You can make suggestions, for instance, by saying "Have you considered?" rather than "You should." (We're not mincing words; there's a real difference in attitude between telling someone what to do and offering suggestions.) You can be more subtle in your approach. For example, instead of sitting Michael down at the kitchen table with a Magic Marker and the classified ads, Randy could simply mention that there's a lot of jobs this week in his particular field. She can offer help—and then graciously back off if Randy refuses.

Second, EXPECT YOUR PARTNER TO BE ACCOUNTABLE FOR HIS ACTIONS. This is the first rule of effective parenting, so it follows that being a "good mother" to your mate requires expecting him to take responsibility for his own life. This is easier said than done. The challenge is to let go and let him do things his way when we're tempted to excuse, rationalize, or fix his mistakes because doing so avoids a fight and makes our own lives easier in the short term. But letting our mate off the hook or covering for him has negative long-term repercussions. He keeps acting like a child, and we're right back where we started, having to act like his mother, when we want to be his friend, lover, and life partner.

Third, RESIST THE TEMPTATION TO CAPITALIZE ON OUR PARTNER'S VULNERABILITY. This may sound harsh, but it's a common scenario that unfolds in this way: We're so hungry for our partner to open up and let us in, that the instant he reveals his softer, more vulnerable side, we're like vultures, pushing him to go further and further in spilling his guts. This is a mistake. When men reveal their vulnerability, they typically need to withdraw a bit before they can "reenter" the relationship. This is useful information. Since men seem to express their vulnerability in brief intervals, followed by a period of withdrawal, the worst thing we can do is seize the opportunity to push our partner to open up even more. When we do this, he, once again, experiences us as his mother, which is both confusing and upsetting to him. He wants to be close to us, but if he feels overly exposed, he feels that we have more power, which causes him to feel impotent. It's a guy thing. An ego thing. Be sensitive to his need to recharge his ego.

Fourth and last, the best way to stop acting like his mother—or prevent his thinking that we're acting like his mother—is to MAKE SURE THAT OUR OWN LIVES ARE SATISFYING AND FULFILLING. The more focused we are on our own growth, career, friendships, and interests, the less likely we are to be overly invested in how our mate "behaves." This, of course, is a double-edged sword. On the one hand, when we're involved in and excited about our own lives, we are less concerned with how our partner conducts his. On the other hand, the happier and more empowered we feel, the more annoying it is to see our partner abdicate responsibility and act like a child. That's when we have to remind ourselves that his life is his life, our life is our life. We have total control over becoming healthy, strong, and responsible for ourselves, and relatively little control over what our mate does or doesn't do. We can, however, take comfort in being a good role model. Hopefully he'll follow in our footsteps.

ON THE BRIGHT SIDE

If you stop acting like his mother, then he's forced to start acting like an adult. Every time you resist the urge to nag, excuse, coddle, or cover for him, he has to become more responsible and accountable for his actions. If you're a mother, you don't need any more children, so this is a real reward. If you don't have children, it's for a reason, which may be that you want an adult male friend, lover, and companion, not someone you have to take care of to this extent. So hold the line. Don't give in to your maternal instincts because you're not doing him, you, or your relationship any favors. Expect him to be an adult, and you may be pleasantly surprised by his rising to the occasion.

If he takes you for granted

I adored my late father-in-law, Lester. He was loving, generous, and competent in any number of ways. After his death, my mother-in-law, Jane, received dozens of notes from people, many of them strangers, expressing appreciation over his having gone miles out of his way to help, whether in getting their business off the ground or being a huge source of support and encouragement. I still miss his daily calls to ask how my current project is coming along, his driving me to the dentist or picking up his two-year-old granddaughter, Zoe, to take her to breakfast, with an orange in his hand to appease her until the food came and two dollars to bribe the waitress to change her diaper.

In short, Lester was a "giver." Except at home. As powerful as he was in the outside world, the minute he'd walk through the door, he turned into the most helpless man on the planet. I recall countless dinners at my in-laws, with Lester sitting at the head of the table and my mother-in-law scurrying around serving the pot roast and noodle pancakes she'd labored over for hours. The instant she'd finally sit down to join us, Lester would immediately pipe up with the same question, as if it were a line out of a play I'd seen dozens of times.

The line was: "Janie, where's the ketchup?" Lester loved ketchup; he put it on everything, including apple pie. Now I'd bet my bottom dollar that Lester knew exactly where the ketchup was. It was right where it always was, on the bottom shelf in the refrigerator, right between the pickles and the low-fat ranch dressing. He could have found it in his sleep. Yet there he'd sit, dinner after dinner, saying, "Where's the ketchup?" which Janie would dutifully fetch for him every single time. Needless to say, my in-laws were in their seventies; their gender roles were defined by their generation, so naturally my efforts to convince Janie not to get up and get the ketchup fell on deaf ears.

You'd think times would have changed. But, no . . . Last week I was invited to dinner at a friend's, where a frighteningly similar scene was reenacted. I watched as my fortyish friend jumped up dozens of times to refill platters while her husband comfortably sat and ate, enjoying the conversation around the table without even so much as offering to help.

Wouldn't it be wonderful to be waited on once in a while—and I *don't* mean getting served breakfast in bed on Mother's Day, but on a regular basis, as most of us do for our partners? Although my friend's husband is a bit of a throwback, many women still complain that their mate displays some version of the "I'm a guy, therefore I deserve to be waited on" syndrome. This attitude isn't always as blatant as sitting at the head of the table, literally waiting to be served. Here's a few more subtle examples: He expects his shirts to be taken to the dry cleaners, then neatly hung in plastic bags in his closet, but would it occur to him to ask if you need anything taken to the dry cleaners and then taking fifteen minutes of his precious time to pick them up? He expects the kids to be quiet while he's watching the Final Four. (Read: You take them to the library or the playground to get them out of his hair.) Or he expects you to be ready for sex when he is, whether or not you're too tired, distracted, have PMS, or just not in the mood.

Ideally, men and women in intimate relationships would naturally serve each other, not as "servants" but just because we love this person so much that we want to do anything we can to make each other happy. Unfortunately, whereas the urge to serve comes easily to women, the same isn't true for men.

Here is a case in point. My upstairs neighbor has the flu. When I run into her in the hallway, she is pale, feverish, sniffling, and on her way out to pick up an antibiotic at the drugstore. I'm rushing as usual, past deadline on a project, late to pick up my daughter from school. Naturally I send her back to bed, promising to return with the filled prescription within the hour, which I do, along with saltines, some Good Earth tea, and this week's *People* magazine.

Believe me, I'm not looking for applause. This is exactly what you and most other women would do, without thinking twice. But here's the killer. As I'm handing her the supplies, I ask her whether Jack, her steady boyfriend, is coming over. "Oh, right," she sneers, caustically. "He called last night to tell me what time he was picking me up for a party, and I told him I was feeling awful, that I couldn't keep anything down, and my temperature was up to 102. And you know what he said?" "What?" I asked, already knowing the answer. "Well, I'll tell you what he didn't say," she replied. "He didn't say, 'Oh, honey, what do you need?' He didn't say, 'I'll be right over with chicken soup and a video.' He said, 'Well, since you're probably not up to going to the party, I'll call you tomorrow to see if you're feeling better,' and then he hung up! Frankly," she continued, "I was too sick to even get angry. But I can tell you this much. If the situation was reversed, I'd have dropped everything to run over there and take care of him."

WHY ARE THEY LIKE THIS?

Before we assume that most men would just as soon step over a bleeding body in the street as stop and ask what they could do, let's take a quick look at the difference between how men and women are raised. Although those of us with male children are making a real effort to teach them to be more giving than their older counterparts, the fact is that most women were brought up to be caregivers—to put other people's needs ahead of their own. (Even some high-level female executives say they end up making the coffee at work even though it falls under the job description of their male assistants.) In contrast, most males have been raised with a certain sense of entitlement and a lack of emphasis on the importance of giving to others, especially if those "others" happen to be the significant women in their lives. To put it bluntly, we were taught to give, and they were taught to take. This doesn't excuse their behavior, but it does explain why they may expect to be waited on.

Their mothers may have doted on them, serving them second helpings while expecting their daughters to clear the table and wash the dishes. Teachers may have given them a break on finals (especially if being on the football team depended on their final grade), and past girlfriends and ex-wives may have spoiled them by giving more than they got, all of which has reinforced men's beliefs that they deserve everything they get. And that they needn't worry about reciprocating.

This conditioning runs deep. While I consider myself a conscious feminist, I catch myself expecting my daughter to help out more than my son, which she's called me on more than once. At first, I justified it by the fact that she's older (but saying "he's my baby" just doesn't fly when your baby is thirteen years old), but I've forced myself to reckon with the fact that I haven't escaped the unconscious belief system that somehow women are here to serve and men are here to receive. I actually have to force myself not to pick up after my son and to insist on his folding the laundry, just as I'd expect my daughter to pitch in and help. But as hard as I try to treat my children equally, the very fact that I have to make an effort reveals my and other women's part in creating and perpetuating this pattern with the men in our lives.

HOW WE MAKE IT WORSE

So, fine. *It's a guy thing.* We were taught to give, and they were taught to receive our endless gifts without giving the same in return. But that doesn't mean we have to keep doing it and doing it and doing it! We may have unwittingly reinforced this pattern early in our relationship; we were so crazy in love we couldn't stop ourselves from making his favorite lasagna from scratch or picking up fresh flowers on the way to his apartment or surprising him by cleaning his bathroom after he left for work. And in the beginning, our partner's efforts to please may have been considerably greater in his attempt to court us, win us, or, let's be honest, get us into bed. In the early stages of romance, men tend to be more attentive, whereas women continue to do the "little things that make a difference" far longer into the relationship.

But that's *our* choice. Waiting on our mate is an intentional act, which may or may not serve us, depending on our motives. I always hesitate to encourage women to give less, since that's part of what makes us so wonderful, plus it gives us pleasure to do lovely things for our mate. But here's the other side: We keep waiting on our partner while waiting for him to reciprocate, which is about as productive as waiting for a florist to show up with a dozen roses just because it's Valentine's Day and we've just finished wrapping the carefully chosen coffee table book on antique cars (his hobby) along with the handwritten poem we spent hours composing. In other words, this is one area in which being a good role model doesn't work. If you think that the more you give to him, the more he'll give back, think again. That's not how the formula works. If anything, there's an inverse relationship between serving our partner and his reciprocating in kind. If he's grown accustomed to us waiting on him, the more we do it, the more he'll expect it to continue. Who can blame him? Think about it: If he were as nice to you as you are to him, wouldn't you come to expect and enjoy such wonderful treatment?

Surprise! You'd think the answer would be yes, but in

fact it's a little more complicated. Another way in which we play into this problem is by not believing that we deserve to be treated as well as we treat our partner, our friends, or our kids. The list could go on and on, but let's keep this within the context of our intimate relationship with our partner.

Whereas men need to shed some of their sense of entitlement, women need to cultivate a little more of it, and what better place to start than with the one person who says he loves you—your mate? We have to really believe, in our heart of hearts, that we have the right to be treated like queens (or at least, not like servants) once in a while. We have to place more value on ourselves. We have to get over thinking that our partner's (and everyone else's) love for us is conditional, that we have to keep giving and giving in order to win their love and approval.

Our need for external approval is another way in which our behavior and attitude enter into the equation. Whether or not we're aware of it, we may be afraid that asking and expecting our partner to serve us will upset the apple cart and potentially push him away. We don't want to expect too much for fear of being disappointed; the less we expect, the safer we are. But we're missing a very important point. One of the best gifts is the gift of receiving. We may know intellectually that a successful love relationship requires give-and-take—that means us taking, too—but deep down, we believe that being a good girlfriend, lover, or wife means bending over backward to please our partner. After all, most of us watched our mothers do it, and even if we try to do a 180-degree turn, we're still carrying around this role model in our mind.

Getting beyond our conditioning means accepting that other people, including our partner, want and need to give, even if his behavior doesn't reflect this. This may not be easy to swallow, but we may, without realizing, be unreceptive to our partner's attempts to serve us. Hang in here with me for a minute while I explain. There are two different aspects of this dynamic, one is his, and the other is ours. His part is that often men don't give because they either don't know what we want or how to give it, or they find us unapproachable on some level. Our part is that we're either running so fast we don't create a space in which our partner can reach us, or we're so angry at him that we give him the message that no matter what he does, at this point, it's simply not enough.

It may or may not be. But before we conclude that he's never going to serve us the way we serve him, we have to be willing to look at two things: First, we need to be honest about our level of receptivity, that is, whether we're genuinely open to our partner's efforts at pleasing us. One of my friends—who for obvious reasons will remain anonymous—made me promise to call one chapter in this book "If he treats the dog better than he treats you," which I thought about and then rejected because her husband knows exactly how to please their dog but hasn't a clue how to do the same for her. Plus, the dog wags its tail in appreciation, whereas my friend may accept her husband's attempts to be there for her, but she's just as likely to mistrust or push him away after years of getting her hopes up and then having them dashed.

Our level of receptivity (and, believe me, I'm hoping, not assuming, that he's trying in his own way) largely depends on how willing we are to trust and forgive our partner for past sins. Trust and forgiveness require the willingness to make a fresh start. Give him the benefit of the doubt unless and until he proves you wrong. Even if it's a stretch, believe that he genuinely wants to please you but doesn't know how.

Moreover, we need to examine our definition of giving. What looks like giving to him may not even seem in the neighborhood to us, which is one of the reasons why men appear clueless when women complain about what's missing in their relationship. Part of what's missing is our understanding of the difference in how men and women give. Again, it's quite simple: Whereas women express love by serving, men do the same by being protective and taking care of their mate.

Need examples of concrete ways in which men give? Fair enough. We already know the myriad ways in which women give, so we needn't go over them again. But the ways in which men give may be harder to identify. Here are a dozen typical examples of how men give by "taking care" of the woman they love:

- fixing things around the house
- providing financial support
- lifting heavy objects
- holding us in their arms
- dropping us off at the door of a restaurant so we don't have to trudge through snow in three-inch heels
- raking the leaves and putting up the storm windows
- saying, "Don't talk to your mother like that" when our kids are out of line
- coaching us through childbirth (Don't compare this to being in labor. Don't even go there!)
- hanging pictures and moving furniture

Okay, I made it to nine, and I'm starting to have to

think too hard, so you take a turn. I'll give you a handicap. Just think of five ways in which your partner "serves" you by taking care of you. Include anything and everything that's offered in a spirit of helpfulness, including caring for the yard, the car, the roof . . . you get the idea.

You may be surprised at how many ways your mate is kind, loving, and generous toward you. Of course, you may also get upset if you can't come up with anything, in which case, try it another way. Remember the last time he did something that pleased you. It can be anything, even if it seems trivial, like asking how your day was at work or giving you a back rub, even if you had to ask. It still counts! This exercise is strictly meant for you to stop and take stock of any ways in which you haven't noticed or realized that your partner is, in fact, giving, even if his effort may be less consistent or his style different from yours.

Even if you're able to identify lots of ways in which your partner pleases you, you may still resent the fact that he appears to expect you to wait on him without doing the same for you. After all, he says he loves you, so why doesn't he treat you the way you deserve to be treated?

WHAT HOOKS US

Lack of reciprocity makes us feel as if we don't matter. A little appreciation would go a long way, yet so many of our efforts go unnoticed. Not only does our partner forget to say "thank you," but he fails to go out of his way to make our lives easier, which doesn't seem like asking very much.

Besides appreciation, we need and deserve a little love

and nurturing. With all we give, how hard would it be for him to anticipate our needs the way we anticipate his, to occasionally put us first? What's really galling is that we give and give, and we're just not getting enough back.

Now, let's get something straight. We're not asking for the moon here; no one (well, no one I know) is expecting extravagant gifts, nightly massages, or a surprise all-expenses-paid Caribbean cruise, with even the baby-sitters arranged, so that all we have to do is lose five pounds in order to fit into our bathing suit. Our partners may *think* we're "high-maintenance" (more about this new handy-dandy women-bashing phrase in chapter 9), that we're impossible to please, but really, most women would be thrilled by the occasional little gift for no reason, encouraged by just once in a while hearing him say, "Gee, you look tired, honey. Let me make dinner tonight." A woman in one of my workshops talked fifteen minutes straight, marveling over the fact that her husband had actually gone to a bookstore and brought home a daily meditation book on menopause when she started having hot flashes. From her level of amazement and delight you would have thought he'd given her diamonds.

I wish I could write a book giving men specific instructions on how to easily please the woman they love. Instead, you'll have to tell him yourself, which brings us to the first step in getting him to be a little more thoughtful and generous.

SIMPLE SOLUTIONS

Before we talk about what *to* do, here's a couple of what *not* to do's if your partner expects you to wait on him and doesn't return the favor. First, NEVER, EVER, LET YOURSELF BE TREATED LIKE A DOORMAT. I repeat: Don't jump through hoops to satisfy his needs. Don't respond to demands. Don't wait on him hand and foot unless he treats you exactly the same way, in which case, you have nothing to worry about in the first place. The point is: I don't care how terrific he is, how much you love him, or how dependent or intimidated you feel. This is purely a matter of personal dignity. To put it bluntly, keep acting like a menial laborer or his personal maid and you'll keep being treated that way. Count on it. Which is why, if you're accustomed to fulfilling his every little wish, it's going to take a little practice to change your behavior.

To make this work, you first have to change your attitude. That is, CHANGE YOUR ATTITUDE TOWARD YOURSELF. The best way to attract your partner's respect is by respecting yourself, which means valuing yourself enough to stop diminishing your self-worth in order to gain his approval or avoid his wrath. And he may indeed get mad. Men who are used to being served can get angry, ornery, and even ugly when we stop treating them like king of the castle. Too bad. If your new behavior provokes your mate's anger, especially if he becomes confrontational or abusive, get out of his way and keep up the good work.

However, DON'T EXPECT A TOTAL CONVERSION. Here's where a little strategy comes in. It's human nature to resist change, so it's going to take some time for your partner to adjust to your sudden change from domestic serf to Fabulous Goddess Who Deserves to Be Treated with Love and Respect. You don't have to make an instant and dramatic transformation; it's perfectly okay—in fact, it's better—to slowly change the program. For example, let's say you've been cleaning up after him for fifteen years, muttering under your breath but doing it all the same. Now he walks in the door and discovers his underwear lying on the floor next to the bed, just where he dropped it; his leftover scrambled eggs congealing on the plate, just where he left it in the sink; and the sports page flung open on the couch, just where he tossed it before leaving for work. "What's going on?" is a fair question for him to ask. "Why is this place such a mess?" isn't a particularly nice way to put it, but given history, who can blame him for expecting you to behave exactly as you've done throughout the entirety of your relationship. Remember: You're reading this book, he isn't. You're the one who has decided to change, whereas he doesn't have any idea as to what's going on.

Here's how to break it to him gently. Don't throw a fit. Don't throw his dirty underwear at him. And DON'T THROW YOUR YEARS OF ACCUMULATED ANGER IN HIS FACE. Go slow and easy. If you want him to know exactly what's going on, simply explain that you've realized you've been cleaning up after him for too long, and you've decided to stop. From now on, he'll have to clean up after himself. If you don't want to get into details, all you have to do is casually remark, "You're right. It is a mess in here. Maybe you should wash your dishes and put the newspaper in the recycling bin." If you want to be direct (and remember: being specific is the most successful approach), sit him down and calmly tell him what you want. Use language such as: "I'd really appreciate it if you'd put your underwear in the hamper when you get up in the morning." Or "Please wash your dishes before you leave for work."

If he retorts with a lame response such as "I don't have time" or "I'm rushing off to work, but you've got plenty of time to . . . ," take a deep breath, smile, and repeat these words to yourself: *I am his beloved, not his servant.* Then repeat your request. Whatever you do, DON'T PICK UP AFTER HIM. You may end up having to look at his dirty dish or step over his underwear for a while, but sooner or later he'll get the idea. Don't give up and don't give in. The biggest mistake women make is that we ask our partner to do something, and when he doesn't, we do it ourselves because we can't tolerate the alternative, in this case, living with his mess. Boom—he's off the hook and we're right back where we started.

If nothing changes, here's what to do: Put his mess in a corner and leave it there until he takes care of it, even if it sits there for weeks. I know you're thinking, Am I supposed to leave disgustingly stinky dishes in the sink for months? No. Put them on his side of the bed or next to his shoes in the closet. Do whatever it takes to get the message across. One woman I know couldn't stand those little white specs scattered on the mirror in the bathroom from her husband's flossing his teeth. After years of cleaning the mirror, she decided to leave them there to see if he'd notice. It took three weeks, but when he could no longer see his own reflection he asked her where the Windex was. (Meanwhile, she put on her makeup and brushed her teeth in front of the mirror in her bedroom.)

There's nothing wrong with helping your mate clean up his act. Remind him once, twice, maybe three times, but after that, stop. If he says that he doesn't know where the dirty laundry goes or how to run the dishwasher (you wouldn't believe how many men try this one), lead him to the hamper and show him how to stack the dishes. Do this calmly and nicely even though it seems ridiculous to have to show a grown man what your six-year-old knows how to do. Just do it. If you're polite, he can't turn this into a fight. If you are patient, eventually he'll run out of excuses and you'll have succeeded in reducing the number of menial tasks you do in order to placate and please him.

As far as getting your mate to wait on you (do nice things for you and go out of his way to please you) once again, you'll have to take some initiative. Here's the key: EDUCATE, DON'T DENIGRATE. Easy translation: Teach your partner how to please you. Instead of berating him for treating you like a piece of furniture, tell him how much it would mean to you if he treated you like a precious object, one that he truly loved and cared for. Here again, specifics work. Before you approach your partner, sit down and think of three or four specific ways in which you would like him to be more thoughtful and nurturing. For example, your list might include: When you make dinner, he washes the dishes. Or you take one night off a week to do whatever you feel like while he cares for the kids. Ask him to bring you an occasional bouquet of fresh flowers or go shopping with you to pick out a dress for his sister's wedding.

You'd be amazed at how well men respond when they're given concrete instructions, not to mention positive reinforcement, which we'll move on to in the next chapter. For now, suffice it to say, the more you thank him, the more he'll give. Every time he does something nice for you, be sure to let him know how much you appreciate his efforts.

In thinking about how you'd like your partner to please you, let your mind wander back to an earlier stage in your relationship, when most likely your mate was more romantic and forthcoming. In the courtship stage, men tend to make romantic gestures; it's that old "conquest thing"—

we get seduced by roses, poetry, and candlelit dinners, which, unfortunately, seem to diminish or disappear entirely once we've settled into a committed relationship. In other words, once he has you, he doesn't think he has to do anything to keep you.

Wrong! And you may be equally guilty of having stopped doing the special things that keep romance alive, so here's a good way to approach this issue. Wait for the right moment (lying in bed, lingering over coffee, sitting on the porch looking at the stars—anytime when stress is at a minimum and there's a feeling of closeness between you) and remind him of what it used to be like. Don't say: "You never bring me flowers anymore." Do say: "I'll never forget our second date, when you called my best friend to find out what my favorite flowers were and showed up with a dozen peach-colored tulips." Don't say: "I can't remember the last time you gave me a back rub." Do say: "You give the best back rubs. I really miss feeling your hands massage me with that special oil we used to have." Men *love* flattery. They like doing what they do well, so give him a list of ways in which he can easily serve you, and keep rewarding him with your genuine appreciation.

Educating and rewarding your partner is certain to yield a certain degree of success, but his efforts may still not be enough to provide all the love, support, and nurturing that's missing from your life. Here's where you have to take responsibility for giving yourself what he can't or won't deliver. We've all heard and said that no one can give you everything, yet many women still look to the man in their life for the majority of the emotional support and physical nurturing they crave. But one of the best gifts you can give yourself is to diversify, to ACCEPT THE FACT THAT

You Have to Go Beyond Your Relationship for Some of What You Need, both by developing other significant relationships and, most of all, by learning to give to *yourself.*

Here are some specific ways to treat yourself well:

- Join a health club and exercise on a regular basis.
- Make time to spend with close friends.
- Treat yourself to a haircut, manicure, facial, or massage.
- Buy yourself flowers. (I'm not kidding. I do it once a week.)
- Attend a class or cultivate a hobby.
- Set aside at least a half hour every day to meditate, read, walk, or do anything else that helps you relax.
- Treat yourself to lunch, dinner, or even just a cup of coffee. Let someone else, even if it's a waiter—wait on you!
- Create rituals that enhance your serenity. For instance, draw a nightly bath, using your favorite oils, lock the door, and light your favorite scented candles while you luxuriate. Make sure your partner and/or children know you are not to be disturbed.

Doing nice things for yourself has two important benefits. First, you enjoy the rewards of nurturing and indulging yourself. Second, your partner sees firsthand how much more relaxed you are (which carries over to how you treat him), which may motivate him to treat you a little better. In either case, what matters is to treat yourself well.

ON THE BRIGHT SIDE

Being nice to your partner is its own reward, just as treating yourself well is its own reward. When we serve our partner because we're just feeling loving, we end up getting at least as much, if not more, pleasure than he does. For example, when we buy someone the perfect gift, we often have as much fun choosing it as they do opening it. Treating ourselves well, to either compensate for or complement our partner's degree of generosity, yields lasting rewards. And when we are good to ourselves, we are less dependent on our partner, so that what he does give comes as a pleasant surprise.

If he says he wants space

Back when Roseanne Barr was developing her Domestic Goddess routine, one of my favorite lines of hers was: "He said he wanted space. So I threw all his belongings on the front yard, locked the door, and said, 'You want space. Here, take the whole yard and the rest of the block, for all I care.'"

"I just need some space, babe." These words have become one of the latest buzz phrases used by men, and they're about as vague and meaningless as our favorite five words, "Men just don't get it."

Would someone please tell me exactly what "I just want some space" means, so that I don't have to interpret, extrapolate, agonize, or fantasize the worst-case scenario, and we all know what I'm talking about. Yes, according to *Cosmo* and other popular magazines aimed mostly at women who are looking for, trying to keep, or trying to figure out whether or not he's really the mythical Mr. Right, the word *space* isn't a reference to NASA; it's a red flag that the man they're romantically involved with is trying to squirm his way out of the relationship.

This may be true in the dating world. Many of us, myself included, have felt that thump in the pit of our stomach and the sense of impending doom when on the receiving end of that icky, awkwardly uttered sentence. If you've ever had this experience, you, too, may shudder when your partner says he wants space. But especially in long-term, committed relationships, these words don't always mean what we think they mean. In fact, they can mean a number of different things, some directly related to you, others having nothing to do with you, including:

- I'm overworked and need some time to myself.
- I'm bored and want a little freedom and adventure.
- I don't know how to deal with a problem we're having, so I'll just invoke the "space" privilege.
- I'm feeling smothered and need to detach.
- I'd rather go fishing than go to your mother's house for another endless Sunday-morning brunch.
- I'm confused about our relationship and need to analyze my feelings.
- I'm feeling pressured and want you to get out of my face.
- I want out, but I don't know how to say it.

Wouldn't it be amazing if men had the self-awareness to know what they're feeling and the courage to express it directly? Most women just want to know the truth. Whatever it is, knowing what's actually going on in our mate's heart and mind is almost always better than having to guess or imagine, since we tend to imagine the worst. Trying to get at the truth often creates another confusing dynamic between women and men. Women prefer (okay, need) clarity (such as, "Would you please tell me exactly where you're at instead of pushing me away or pretending everything's okay when it obviously isn't"), whereas men will go miles out of their way to avoid having to articulate their real feelings. This is one of the most prevalent ways in which couples get stuck, because the more obscure men are, the harder we try to get them to define and describe their inner emotional terrain, which they seem patently unable or unwilling to do. And naturally, the harder we push, the more they withdraw, which makes them want—guess what?—*more space!*

WHY ARE THEY LIKE THIS?

As a woman trying to get at the underlying motivations for this particular behavior, I'm at somewhat of a handicap. Personally, I'm so self-revealing that understanding and explaining this one has me somewhat stumped. So as to assure myself that I'm on the right track, I checked out my assumptions with several men—friends, friends' husbands, ex-boyfriends, and my next-door neighbor, who was out mowing his lawn—all of whom confirmed my reasoning.

Reason Number 1: FEAR OF CONFRONTATION. Apparently men would sooner kill a bat or change a tire on a dark highway in the middle of nowhere than have to talk about their feelings of needing more privacy, time alone, or especially about feeling confused and ambivalent about their intimate relationship.

Reason Number 2: FEAR OF SAYING THE WRONG THING. Here's yet another interesting gender difference: Women tend to blurt out their feelings (sometimes prematurely or before they're well thought out), while men may wait, hesitate, or refuse to say how they're feeling unless and until they're absolutely certain. This is about accountability, or in other words, men's terror that anything they say will be etched in stone and that we will hold them to their word.

Reason Number 3: FEAR OF HURTING US. I find this one particularly fascinating. Nothing hurts more than having to wonder what our partner means when he says "I want space," yet they actually believe that they're protecting us by censoring themselves. Will someone please tell them to just spit it out? We may be vulnerable, but we're not about to go to pieces just because our partner is feeling cramped, confused, or even seriously rethinking our relationship. It's okay!!! What *isn't* okay is to ignore, avoid, or talk around it, which makes us feel crazy, needy, and insecure.

Reason Number 4: FEAR OF INTIMACY. "I need space" as often as not is code for "This is getting too emotionally intense." Men typically "go away" when they feel emotionally overwhelmed or at risk of losing their independence and autonomy. This is extremely confusing for women. It's another one of those "guy things." Just as we're feeling especially close to our partner—we've had a really personal conversation, we've finally agreed to buy a house together, we've had sex two nights in a row—and what does he do? Instead of wanting more, he runs for the door! This is predictable, so we can anticipate it, which we'll explore further on in this chapter.

These four reasons are what most men mean when they say they need space. But, of course, there's always the possibility that what he means is that he's actually reached a point of wanting the relationship to end. But assuming your mate's need for space has more to do with the other reasons outlined above, there are many simple and practical ways to deal with this issue. We can give him space, we can insist on his defining *space,* we can take some space, we can be proactive in a number of ways, but first, let's take a look at our part in this particular dilemma.

HOW WE MAKE IT WORSE

Before we take an honest look at our part in our mate's wanting space, let me make one thing perfectly clear: Our behavior, attitudes, or actions don't force him into seeking asylum, nor are we responsible for his inability to be straightforward about what he wants. Having said this, there are ways in which we may contribute or even provoke him to withdraw. Likewise, how we react when he says he wants space may inadvertently worsen this problem.

How? For starters, we may balk or give our mate a hard time when he takes time for himself that doesn't include us. There are lots of good and understandable reasons why we may resist or resent his desire for space. Here's a few: His taking space may rankle us if we're desperately in need of a break and feel that it's our turn to get away. (This is especially infuriating when his going away means we're left alone with the kids.) We may resent his taking space when we're counting on his company or have already made conflicting plans, which we either have to cancel or act on alone.

Mostly, we may have a hard time graciously "giving him space" when we sense that what he's *really* doing is avoiding having to confront difficult issues existing between us.

That's when we get scared. Our fear and anxiety are

expressed by us pushing, pouting, or interrogating our partner instead of staying cool and giving him his space. Here's another difference between the genders: Whereas our partner may genuinely not know what's going on with himself and therefore is reluctant to talk about it, women are much more in touch with feelings. Call it women's intuition. Call it greater self-awareness or that intangible sixth sense that many women seem to possess. Whatever we call it, the net result is that *he's* saying "everything's fine" and *we* know it's not, which is one of the most crazy-making aspects of being in a relationship with a man.

This is a no-win situation; we have the insight that often enables us to "know" our partner better than he knows himself, yet acting on this instinct by telling him he's scared, overwhelmed, and avoiding his real feelings is the kiss of death. We've arrived at yet another "guy thing." They stubbornly refuse to accept our useful input; it's the emotional equivalent of their insistent refusal to ask directions when they're two hours late and twenty miles off course. Because of this, it's wise to be careful in our approach; casually inquiring as to our partner's plans, feelings, or needs is fine, as long as we don't fall into the trap of interrogating him. Asking too many questions is easily interpreted as putting him on the witness stand. For example, if you ask your partner why he needs the weekend to himself and he replies that he wants to go camping with his three best male friends, accept his explanation, tell him to have a great time, and then get busy making your own weekend plans. You don't have to ask him the exact location of the camping site, nor do you need to find his fishing pole, remind him to take along rain gear, or send along your famous home-baked brownies. Remember: He wants space. That means, let him go and remove yourself from the picture, which he'll appreciate far more than your well-meaning efforts to enhance his vacation.

Assuming we're able to get to (or sense) the real reason he needs his "space," we have several ways to react. Going back to the reasons listed earlier, for example, if our partner needs space because he just wants some downtime to be by himself, then there's every reason to grant his wish. (Assumption: He's looking for an evening or a weekend, not three months in the Caribbean.) If he's asserting his independence because he feels pressured or is scared that you are getting too clingy or dependent, then you need to back off. It doesn't matter whether or not you're actually being possessive or he's just feeling suffocated; either way, pushing is the worst thing you can do. Likewise, if our partner is indicating that he needs space because he's struggling with his feelings about us—or, for that matter, anything else—we sometimes make the mistake of prodding, coaxing, or even forcing him to reveal himself before he's ready. Again, we undermine ourselves by asserting our agenda (insisting that he comply with our timing or need for immediate dialogue), which only increases his desire to escape.

Here's the bottom line: Whether our mate wants space for an innocuous reason that doesn't threaten our relationship or because he's avoiding dealing with issues, patience and restraint are our best tools. But backing off is a real challenge, given our emotional reaction to the statement "I want space."

WHAT HOOKS US

He says "I just want some space" and we hear "I don't want to be with you." Unless we are incredibly secure in our relationship, this sentence, whether expressed gently or belligerently, in a sideways or straightforward manner, pushes our "Oh, no. Maybe he's not in love with me anymore" button. If our relationship is going along swimmingly we may be less freaked out but still a little miffed that he'd rather putter around in the basement than go garage-sale hopping with us. If our relationship is rocky, the words "I want space" are sure to send us into an emotional tailspin.

It's natural to imagine having to initiate divorce proceedings or place a personal ad when the situation is nowhere near that dire. This is a protective response. Our fear that "space" is the harbinger of worse things to come isn't necessarily well grounded. Yes, our partner may be indicating that he needs some separation, but that can be either positive or negative, depending, in large part, on how we play out this particular dynamic.

SIMPLE SOLUTIONS

DON'T PANIC! That's the first and most important thing to remember if and when your mate uses the *S* word (as differentiated from the *I* word, which we'll discuss in chapter 9). Don't assume that just because he turns down your regular Friday-night "date" in favor of going bowling with his buddies, he's losing interest, having an affair, or having a midlife crisis. While I rarely, if ever, encourage women not to take something personally, in this case we may jump to conclusions, taking our partner's behavior personally when it's not.

Taking it personally means interpreting his need for space as a reflection of his love and commitment, or to be more exact, as a sign that he's less interested in us. We make ourselves miserable by blaming ourselves: For instance, you may look at yourself in the mirror, glare at the fifteen pounds you've gained, and think, Why would he want to have a romantic night with someone who looks like this? Or you've been awfully crabby lately, no wonder he wants to work on his car instead of listening to you whine. Or lately you've been so exhausted you've barely had the energy to talk about the weather, much less be a stimulating dinner partner, so of course he's thrilled to go away with his friends and have a little excitement and adventure.

Instead of jumping to conclusions, GET INFORMATION. Clarity is one of the best ways to reduce panic and apprehension. If your mate says he wants space, ask him to elaborate. The four words "What do you mean?" are the best way I've found to get information without sounding pushy or paranoid. It's amazing how well this question works, especially when asked in a casual, nonchalant tone of voice. "Oh, really?" is another effective reply, but only if you're not being sarcastic. Both of these responses are successful because they neutralize potential defensiveness in our mate. We're simply asking him to fill us in, without confronting him in any way that can be interpreted as aggressive or intrusive, which increases the likelihood of getting the information we're seeking without the exchange turning into a conflict.

The third simple solution is to GIVE HIM THE SPACE HE WANTS. Here's where situational ethics enter the picture. There are situations in every relationship in which taking space is appropriate and other times when it's not. For example, there's no reason in the world why your partner shouldn't go skiing for the weekend just because you're unhappy about spending Saturday night alone. On the other hand, you don't have to read Miss Manners to know that if his ski trip happens to fall on your anniversary, conflict with your annual work conference, or fall on the same two days your daughter is competing in the state gymnastic finals, then you have every right to say no.

As always, it's smart to CONSIDER HOW TO SAY NO. Often our first instinct is to come on too strong, especially if our saying no has provoked an argument in the past. Consequently, a good rule of thumb is to wait a full minute, so you don't blow up in his face. Take a deep breath, repeat to yourself, Be nice. Just say what you need to say, and then tell him that this particular weekend doesn't work and explain why. Emphasize the fact that you understand he may be disappointed and suggest another weekend that would be more convenient for everyone.

If he refuses to postpone his plans, TRY TO REACH A COMPROMISE, perhaps his going for part of the time and then cutting his weekend short in order to be home in time for some of the festivities. Of course, there's always the possibility that he may flat out refuse, in which case, go ahead and get mad. But be sure you're being fair. He may be acting like a selfish jerk, or he may actually be in a bind, for instance if the weekend involves five other guys and they've spent weeks coordinating their schedules. However, this begs the question: Then how come you're just finding out about this now?

IF YOU'RE ANGRY, SAY SO. Don't pout, don't threaten, and don't retaliate. Simply express your anger, and let him know what it will take for you to get over it. Again, think before you act. You may need time. You may need an apology. You may need his promise to make it up to you by taking you out for a special anniversary dinner on Monday, or you may just be mad until you're done being mad. That's okay. We need to express our anger when it's happening, rather than repressing it and either imploding or exploding later, and our mate needs to experience the consequences of his actions.

Finally, make sure that you are taking the space, the time, and making the necessary arrangements to nurture yourself. We're far less likely to resent our partner's wanting space when we're nourishing ourselves with friendship, exercise, solitude, and any other sources of pleasure and replenishment. Taking space empowers us, reminds us that we're perfectly capable of fulfilling ourselves in a variety of ways, as well as strengthening our relationship.

If your relationship is tenuous, time alone gives each of you greater perspective and often makes you more grateful for what you have. If your relationship is in pretty good or even great shape, taking space can only enhance the time you spend together.

ON THE BRIGHT SIDE

His taking space gives you the go-ahead to take some space of your own. And believe me, you need and deserve some time alone to rest, reflect, and replenish yourself. Quit fighting it! You may have a thousand reasons why you can't afford to take a vacation, take one night off for yourself, or even an hour just to take a long stroll around the neighborhood. Here's the second perk: When you and your partner each take space, you come back together with more to offer each other. Often this results in both of you not taking each other for granted so much and being more grateful for what you have, both separately and as a couple.

6

If he doesn't take your needs, time, and schedule into consideration

———◆———

Thank God it's Friday! You've had a long, hard week at work, and you're really looking forward to a relaxing, maybe even romantic night at home. You run to the video store and rent the movie he's wanted to see, then stop and pick up his favorite Szechwan noodles and mu-shu pork. You get home, take a shower, and change into comfortable sweats, enjoying the half hour or so before he'll be home. Forty-five minutes pass and you're starting to wonder what's taking him so long. Another twenty minutes go by, then the phone rings. "Hi, babe," he says, "what's going on?" Trying to keep the edge out of your voice, you say, "I'm just hanging, waiting for you to get home." "Oh," he replies, "a bunch of us are going out for drinks. I'll probably be home around midnight, okay?"

OKAY? No. *Not okay at all!* There goes your evening. Plus, what in the world is he thinking, making plans at the last moment for Friday night without consulting you, considering you, and worst, without inviting you to come? The very least he could do is check out your plans for the evening and give you a little notice so that you're not left alone on a Friday night, sitting on the couch eating take-out, and watching the video *he* wanted to see. Sure, you could invite a friend over or go out yourself, but it's a little late, and besides, now you're in a bad mood and don't feel like doing anything.

In my workshops I've heard numerous variations on this theme.

Example 1: Terry's been involved with Rick for three years. They have a standing Saturday night date. Terry is excited about this weekend's plans, which include spending Saturday with their friends Bill and Mary on their boat, and then having a barbecue on their new deck. She's especially looking forward to this weekend because the weather report says it will be ninety-five degrees and sunny, plus she's just lost two more pounds and has a great new bathing suit with a matching sarong that she's dying to wear.

Friday night Rick calls. Terry reminds him to be at her house by noon on Saturday. There's a long pause, then Rick sheepishly says that he's really sorry but he forgot to mention that he's going out of town for the weekend to visit his parents. He'll probably be pretty beat, but he'll try to call Sunday night to say hi.

There are a number of things Terry wants to say right now, like "You're doing *what?*" or "Oh, great. Am I supposed to go out to Bill and Mary's myself?" but at the moment she's speechless. Just two days ago they'd talked about how much fun it would be to go out on the boat, and now this? Terry is angry, disappointed, and hurt, but she says, "Oh. Have a nice time," before hanging up and bursting into tears.

Example 2: Wendy really needs a night off. Her husband, Kurt, has just returned from a five-day business trip; their son, Ben, has had a virus the whole time, keeping Wendy up three nights in a row. She's barely dragged herself through work and had to take time off to take Ben to the doctor. Wendy's sister calls and invites her out for dinner and a movie. All Wendy really wants is to crawl under the covers and sleep for forty-eight hours, but she knows if she's home, she'll end up having to take care of Ben. She tells her husband she's going out, would he please make sure Ben eats dinner (it's on the stove) and is in bed by nine. "I'm playing poker tonight," says Kurt. "Maybe you can have dinner with Lisa tomorrow." Wendy loses it and screams, "I've been taking care of a sick kid for the past seven days and you think you're going out to play poker?" They end up in an argument during which Kurt storms out and doesn't return until after midnight.

What's the deal? The deal is that sometimes our mate operates as if we don't exist, going about his business without taking our needs, our time, and our schedule into consideration. And this *is* a matter of consideration. Let's call a spade a spade; this sort of behavior is just plain rude, no matter how you look at it. Assuming you confer with your mate before making plans (this is a fair assumption, given how most women operate), it's natural to expect him to do the same, but once again, expectations don't necessarily match reality.

Whether or not this is a major issue depends, in part, on the nature of your relationship, including whether you live together or apart, whether or not you have children (in which case, practical logistics enter in), the quality of your communication, whether you normally discuss plans ahead of time or check in with each other on the spot, and whether or not it's assumed that certain nights or weekend times are spent together unless something special comes up. In addition, how big an issue this is depends on whether it's a first-time offense, something he does once in a while, or a continuing pattern in your relationship. But regardless of whether this behavior is uncharacteristic or an ongoing problem, it's helpful to explore why some men act this way.

WHY ARE THEY LIKE THIS?

Let's start by giving men the benefit of the doubt. His making plans without telling you may simply be a matter of poor communication between the two of you. There is the possibility that he is so busy, distracted, flaky, or out to lunch that he actually spaces out on plans he's been apprised of. There's also the possibility that you're being too vague and mention plans in passing without explicitly telling him when, where, and with whom. Although you shouldn't have to run your relationship like a business, some men truly need their social schedule spelled out, through verbal reminders and written memos. I agree, this is pathetic, but again, your goal is to deal with the particular man in your life, which may require communicating in a clearer, more formal manner.

Men may also make plans without informing or asking their partner because they're used to being single. Even men who have been married or involved in a committed relationship for a long time may still struggle to think of themselves as part of a couple, instead of an individual who doesn't need to account to anyone. Although I hate to keep pointing my finger at cultural conditioning, we have to give men a little rope here in that they've been raised to value autonomy, whereas women are brought up to seek intimacy. To put it another way, men are raised to be independent and unfettered, whereas women are raised to think of themselves in relation to others, whether it's their friends, children, family members, or mate. The net result: Even the most committed man may have to make a conscious effort to think of himself as part of a couple, and in the most extreme cases he may consciously or unconsciously resent or rail against intimacy and mutuality.

Here's how this plays out. Men, regardless of how evolved they may be, often struggle with an intense need to protect their independence and autonomy. They may be aware of this enough to express it in words, like my friend David, who admits, "I adore my wife, but there are times when we get so close I have this urge to run away. It's not rational. I just get this uncomfortable feeling that I'm going to get swallowed up and somehow lose a part of myself that's just mine."

This attitude is also reinforced within the culture; think about all the weddings you've attended where the groom is given toasts such as, "Kiss your freedom good-bye" or "Another great guy bites the dust." The ritual "bachelor party," typically a drunken "last supper" complete with a stripper, is a cultural rite of passage in which the groom is jokingly (or maybe not so jokingly) urged to savor his final, fleeting hours of freedom, as if getting married is tantamount to going off to boot camp or starting a prison term. No wonder men associate intimate relationships with loss of freedom and feel as if they must fight to retain any and all shreds of independence so as not to feel or be seen as being "beaten"—the term my teenaged daughter and her friends use to describe guys who are head over heels in love.

Leslie, a woman I saw in counseling, described this phenomenon firsthand. Leslie had been married before, whereas at forty-seven, her boyfriend, Seth, had been involved in several serious love relationships, but none that lasted longer than two or three years. Says Leslie, "On our third date Seth and I went to a movie. During the previews, he said he wasn't feeling great and needed to go to the bathroom. Twenty minutes later, he hadn't returned. I went to the men's room and yelled his name, then asked a passing man to go in and check to see if Seth was all right, but he wasn't in there. Now I was worried. I walked outside the movie theater, located on a corner in a busy commercial part of Minneapolis, and paced up and down the street, looking for a sign of him. After about ten minutes, I saw him casually crossing the street and walking toward me. "Where were you?" I asked. "Oh," he nonchalantly replied, "I decided to go into Calhoun Square to buy a pair of sunglasses."

Leslie was stunned. "Can you believe it?" she asked. "We're on a date and he wanders off to buy sunglasses without it even occurring to him that I'm sitting in the movie theater wondering if he's dead. Naturally, by this time I could have cared less about seeing the movie, so we went for a cup of coffee to talk about what had happened. He apologized and explained that he hadn't been in a relationship for a while, so he'd "kind of, sort of wandered off, temporarily forgetting that he was on a date with me."

According to Leslie, Seth apologized profusely and insisted his behavior had nothing to do with his romantic interest in her. She accepted his apology but inwardly wondered if his "temporary amnesia" was his way of expressing ambivalence about getting involved.

Sometimes it's hard to tell the difference between obliviousness and "acting out." I was recently interviewed for an article in *Cosmo* about men taking women for granted. The writer asked my opinion of the following real-life scenario. Nan, a woman interviewed for the article (all names were fictitious), was furious because she had planned an elaborate party at a local restaurant to celebrate her husband, Paul's, thirty-fifth birthday. It wasn't a surprise party; her husband knew exactly what time he was expected to show up. In what she describes as one of the most "infuriating and mortifying nights of her life," Nan entertained her dozens of guests for over two hours while waiting for Paul to show up. He never did. Late that night Paul returned home to face Nan's fury. He sheepishly explained that he had been playing pool with two friends and had totally lost track of time, for which he was so, so sorry. He wanted to know how he could make it up to her. Nan wanted an expert's opinion, torn between the impulse to tell her husband to go to hell and chalking his behavior up to, what she called, his "absent-minded professor" personality. After sharing this anecdote, the writer from *Cosmo* asked whether I thought Paul was genuinely contrite and couldn't "help" his forgetfulness or whether he was actually a schmuck who was either blatantly or subconsciously trying to sabotage their relationship.

The truth is: *It doesn't really matter.* Remember: What counts is behavior, regardless of the underlying motivations. This all-too-common scenario—men acting out by making and/or breaking plans without taking their partners' feelings into consideration—is patently unacceptable. Staying late at work without calling, going out with the "boys" when the two of you are expected at his parents' house for dinner, or scheduling a business trip that conflicts with your son's high school graduation and could easily be postponed, are all immature ways of "acting out" or expressing the sentiment "don't think you own me," when all you expect is communication and common decency. Before we explore strategies for combating this behavior, let's take a look at how we may be accepting, encouraging, or even promoting our partner's behavior.

HOW WE MAKE IT WORSE

There are two primary ways in which we play into this pattern. The first is related to our tendency to act as social director in our relationship. Typically, women assume responsibility for making dates with friends, handling holiday arrangements with relatives, organizing kids' activities, and all the other plans that fall into the category of social, entertainment, and recreational events. Women tend to keep the social calendar, which is fine, except for one thing: We may not always check with our partner before orchestrating social dates. Or we may make relatively loose and informal plans, contingent on checking them out with our partner. If or when he says no we may end up feeling awkward and caught in the middle, having to explain ourselves to family or friends. Or we may just make plans and assume it's fine with him, only to discover that he's busy or disinterested or is totally opposed to spending his Memorial Day weekend at a cabin with a few of our coworkers, even though he says he really enjoys their company.

Another way we sabotage ourselves is by being presumptuous or bossy about making plans. While you may be totally accustomed to making plans without consulting him or just telling him after the fact (after all, this may have been going on for years), this is a setup for disaster for both you and your mate. Despite your best intentions, making "executive decisions" is counterproductive. Even if you continue to assume the role of social director, be sure to get your mate's okay before agreeing to mutual plans. Failing to consult with him first gives him implicit permission to rebel, "forget," or make conflicting plans without informing you. And we set ourselves up by being left in the lurch or having to apologize or make excuses to friends. Our part in being a respectful partner is to consider his feelings as well, by being sure to involve and include him in making plans rather than presuming that whatever's fine with us will be fine with him.

We may worsen the situation by appearing overly needy, dependent, or intrusive when he makes plans and tells us at the last moment or doesn't tell us at all. Here it's important to make a distinction between an occasional slip and a recurring pattern. If your mate does this once or twice, it's fairly easy to solve this problem, which we'll get to in a moment, but if he continually treats you this way, then more serious intervention is in order. Either way, it's in our own best interest to be conscious of how we react. Sometimes things come up at the last minute, in which case we need to give our mate a little slack. But even if our partner has plenty of notice and still screws up, we need to be careful of our tendency to express our anger and discontent by blaming, shaming, or being nosy about where he's been and what he's up to.

Granted, he *is* to blame. Certainly he should be ashamed

of acting rudely. And, without a doubt, you have the right to know why he's worrying you needlessly, blowing you off, and where in the world he's been until after eleven when he said he'd be home by eight. Several smart and productive strategies can be used that don't reinforce his typical male response, which may or may not be verbally expressed as: "Why are you sitting around waiting for me?" or "Get a life!" or "I don't have to answer to you every time I do something that doesn't include you." Keep in mind that this isn't actually the point; all you're asking is for him to communicate and be respectful of the fact that you do have a life, and maybe, just maybe, you have better things to do than worrying about whether he's gotten into a car accident or waiting around when you could be enjoying yourself. But even the strongest, most assertive women may fall into the trap of whining, complaining, or interrogating instead of calling our partner on his behavior and asking him to clean up his act. Here's why:

WHAT HOOKS US

Most, if not all, women place a high value on taking other people's feelings into consideration. We go out of our way—sometimes too far out of our way—to make sure that we're being thoughtful and sensitive to everyone in our lives, including, and especially, our mate.

So obviously we get angry when we're treated rudely. And we should get mad! Remember the scene in the movie *Network* when one of the main characters screams out the window in the middle of New York City, "I'm mad as hell and I'm not going to take it anymore!"? Lots of us feel this way, but we don't know what to do about our anger, since it doesn't seem as if expressing it changes anything or gets us anywhere. So we end up seething and suppressing our anger instead of expressing it productively.

There's another, even more significant, way in which this issue emotionally hooks us. We feel hurt because we interpret his behavior as a sign that he's not as invested in our relationship as we are. We don't make plans for ourselves without telling him. For that matter, we are more likely to make our plans around him, making our relationship our first priority, either arranging social activities that involve him or using the time when he's busy or out of town to plan a "girls' night out."

This isn't just a matter of manners, it actually has to do with the value we place on mutuality. Given our busy schedules and stress-filled, demanding lives, we know how important it is to make time for our relationship. The last thing we'd do is intentionally exclude him or pass up an opportunity to spend quality time together.

Guess what? *He doesn't think the same way.* If our mate makes plans without telling or including us, it's not necessarily a reflection of his love or level of commitment. Again, this doesn't excuse rudeness, but it's important to understand so that instead of being mired in anger and hurt, we can try some of these solutions and at the very least, give him a chance to come through.

SIMPLE SOLUTIONS

The first simple solution is to Ask Rather Than Tell Your Mate About Any Invitations That Include Him. We can avoid potential "selective memory loss" by actively involving him in decision making, instead of letting him be a passive bystander. One useful strategy is to set a time each week to talk about upcoming invitations and possible plans. There are three agenda items for each week's meeting: your plans; his plans; and mutual plans. The smart move is to begin by asking him to tell you any plans he's made or is thinking of making, either with or without you. Letting him go first is a small sacrifice that implies you are open to anything he wants to do, whether or not it includes you.

Next, TELL HIM YOUR PLANS. Don't ask. Tell. Another mistake women make is that we ask permission rather than simply stating our plans without justifying or defending them. Women, especially those who have children, tend to feel and act apologetic when they take any time off, even though our partner waltzes off to his weekly bowling league without giving it a second thought. Karen, the head ob-gyn nurse in an extremely busy city hospital, says, "When Mark wants to go out, he just says he's going. The rare times I'm invited to a movie or want to just get out of the house for the night I feel as if I have to give him fifteen reasons why I should be able to leave him home with the kids, and even then, I still make dinner and lay out their pajamas before I walk out the door."

Enough with the guilt!! We have every right—in fact, it's essential—to make plans of our own and enjoy them without giving a thirty-minute closing argument on where we're going, why it's important, why we deserve to go . . . We just do!!!

Once you and your mate have each brought up your individual plans for the week, bring up any mutual social activities that are in the making. Remember: If you're the "social director," make sure to present potential plans without already having accepted them and without pressuring your partner to comply. (One good strategy is to nominate him social director for a month, and see how he handles it!)

Once again, IT'S TIME TO NEGOTIATE. Both of you may want to do something on the same night, and if you're parents, you'll have to agree on getting a baby-sitter or one of you staying home. Now there are seven nights in the week, so the two of you should be able to take turns without either of you having to cancel. You may also have to negotiate if you have conflicting plans; for instance, you may want your partner to accompany you to your best friend's art gallery opening on the same night he has tickets to a basketball game. This situation calls for compromise, and here's how to do it. If something is extremely important to either of you, then say so. Make it an invitation, or better yet, a request. Relationships would improve exponentially if both partners could occasionally say "Please do this for me, just because it really matters," which sounds easy, but most of us hesitate either because we loathe having to ask, we don't want to start an argument, or we've been rejected one too many times and aren't about to make ourselves that vulnerable again. But the ability to make genuine requests is a valuable relationship tool. Experiment with it, and you may be surprised at your partner's willingness, even eagerness, to please you when you ask in a way that enables him to look like a great guy.

More likely than not, you may also come up against your mate's resistance to participate in certain social activities. Some social activities fall into the "obligatory" category; for instance, Thanksgiving, your son's piano recital, or your sister's bridal dinner aren't negotiable. Tell him firmly that he's expected to be there and don't take no for an answer. If he whines, walk out of the room. If he refuses to go, go yourself and don't make excuses for him. Remember: His behavior isn't a reflection of you, although it's certainly awkward and embarrassing when our partner doesn't show up, especially at family functions.

Once the two of you have discussed your individual and mutual plans, AGREE ON WHO'S DOING WHAT, WHEN, AND WHERE. Then get out your calendar and put it in writing. (Research in the educational field has proven that writing something down dramatically increases the information being etched into memory), so hand him the red marker and have him be the secretary.

Your weekly meeting will diminish the likelihood of his making plans without telling you in advance. But there are always things that pop up suddenly, that can't be anticipated, which brings us to the next strategy: agreeing on a rule of thumb for making and communicating spur-of-the-moment plans. A simple, fair rule is: We'll give each other twenty-four hours' notice if we want to make plans (that's plenty of time for either of you to accommodate changes and make good use of your time), but if something unexpected comes up, we'll promise to call immediately, and whenever possible, check it out with each other. I say "whenever possible" because sometimes sudden changes in plans, particularly ones that are work related, are unforeseeable and unavoidable, so it's important to factor this in. But in general, your partner should be able to keep his part of the bargain, especially if you emphasize the fact that you just want the simple courtesy of a phone call within a reasonable amount of time. You can explain this by using an example such as, "If you feel like going out for a drink after work, please don't call me from the bar at nine o'clock with some long story or avoid calling me at all because you're scared I'll be mad. All I want is for you to call me or leave a message by five so that I don't expect you home for dinner or wait for you when I could be doing something else." Give him the words if you have to—and you might. If you make it easy for him to communicate without fear of your disapproval or disappointment, he'll be much more likely to act like a responsible adult instead of a teenager who stays out past curfew and doesn't call because he is afraid of getting grounded.

Earlier in this section I promised to offer a simple solution for dealing with those men who, no matter how easy you make it, are chronically rude about communicating plans. Here's my suggestion: STOP WAITING AROUND. We're entering into more difficult territory, which requires more definitive action on your part. Severe as this may sound, and sad as it might be, if you choose to be with a man who doesn't take your time, energy, and needs into account, then you'll have to adjust your expectations and start making solo plans, without waiting for him to change.

This isn't the end of the world, and it needn't be a relationship breaker. There are couples who are attached at the hip, as well as many who find a balance between going off on their own and doing things together. There are also couples who, for the most part, operate independently, such as couples who have successful long-distance relationships or spouses who live in different parts of the country and commute back and forth. So if you need to start becoming more independent, don't necessarily think that this means your relationship is in trouble. On the contrary, getting involved in social activities on our own is something that all women could benefit from. While it's wonderful to share time with our partner, it can be extremely pleasurable and empowering to pursue our own interests, without him at our side. In fact, sometimes having him with us is a drag, particularly if he doesn't want to be there and makes us miserable, ruining what could be a perfectly lovely experience. Women who attend a weekly book club, take a night class, work out by themselves at the gym, or meet girlfriends (or male friends—no need to be sexist here) for dinner inevitably say that these times on their own, away from their relationship, are fun and stimulating. Again, remember that you're not doing this as retribution but rather as a way to meet your own needs, which each of us is responsible for whether we're single or in a relationship.

If you've tried all the suggestions above and still find yourself waiting around for him, then it's time to Get a Life! No one's making you sit by the phone or feel sorry for yourself, watching reruns and eating last night's leftovers. If your partner can't agree to or keep his agreement to follow the house rules, give him fifteen minutes leeway, and then get off your butt and do something for yourself. Whether you crawl under the covers with a great book or put on some eyeliner and push yourself out the door to go to the all-night market or visit a friend, it's up to you to make the most of your time—even if he doesn't seem to value it.

You have to value it, and that means taking action. You'll feel better, and there's a potential perk: When he comes home and finds your note saying "Sorry. I waited for a while, but when you didn't call I decided to go out," he'll eventually start to notice that you're perfectly capable of entertaining yourself and may start paying more attention to how and when he makes and communicates his plans. There's no guarantee, but regardless of his response, you'll feel less resentful and more confident of your capacity to get what you want.

ON THE BRIGHT SIDE

All this can lead to two potential positive outcomes. First, if you follow the simple strategies I've outlined, you have a greater chance of increasing your partner's involvement in making plans and lessening the likelihood of his going off on his own without consulting you or taking you into consideration. Second, if these strategies are unsuccessful, then take comfort in knowing that you can't be too independent. Every new, interesting, and satisfying activity you involve yourself in—whether it's spending time with friends, taking a class, or joining a health club—can only enhance and improve the quality of your life. Letting your partner's schedule dictate your choice keeps you from pursuing your passions. Your best bet is to keep cultivating mutually fun and engaging activities with your mate while simultaneously broadening your own interests and activities.

7

If he's more about having sex than about making love

———————◆———————

This chapter merits a number of subtitles, including:

- If he wants sex more or less often than you do
- If he hasn't noticed how often you fake orgasm
- If he treats you too roughly or too gently
- If he goes too fast (and hasn't heard about foreplay)
- If he expects you to be sexual when you're not getting along
- If he falls asleep five minutes after he climaxes
- If he hasn't a clue how to please you

I don't know where to start! The topic of sex and lovemaking is so broad that it deserves its own book, and of all the issues discussed in this book, it's the most complex. In this more than any other aspect of intimate relationships, there are various interwoven issues at play. The quantity and quality of our lovemaking is directly related to the emotional health of our relationship and vice versa. We can't deal with one without talking about the other.

In my work with couples, I've discovered that regardless of what "issues" are presented during sessions, scratch the surface and sexual problems almost always emerge. Lovemaking is a litmus test for how the rest of our relationship is going. It's rare for a couple to have a terrific relationship and a lousy sex life. Their lovemaking may lack luster, variety, or be too infrequent, due to stress and other situational factors, but usually they're in sync, and that's all that counts. If both partners are satisfied, then their sexual relationship is in fine shape. Conversely, when a couple is struggling with serious problems, their lovemaking usually suffers as well, either becoming less frequent, less passionate, or less satisfying in any number of ways. Some couples manage to have sex (as opposed to making love), even when their relationship is shaky. It may be the "best part" of their relationship, but ultimately, women typically feel discontented and uncomfortable when they are feeling emotionally disconnected. So it's utterly impossible to separate the issue of sexuality from other important aspects of our intimate relationship.

Just as we can't talk about lovemaking in a vacuum, we can't possibly solve every conceivable sexual problem that couples struggle with. We can, however, explore the most universal themes. In reviewing the subtitles listed above, one common thread emerges, which for the case of simplicity, comes down to this: Once again, *he just doesn't get it*—in this case, for a myriad of reasons, he just doesn't "get" what it takes to turn you on.

I refuse to accept or promote the concept that men are

insensitive or ineffectual lovers because they're selfish pigs and only concerned about their own pleasure. I truly believe that the majority of men want to please their partner and would love to know how.

Lack of sexual fulfillment between men and women is one of the saddest, most disturbing, and far too prevalent issues. Lovemaking should—and can—be one of the sweetest, most exciting, and joyous ways in which we connect with our partner. Holding, kissing, fondling, and giving and receiving pleasure are at minimum pleasurable and at times can even achieve a state of holiness, in which we reach heights of ecstasy and communion.

So where does it go awry? How does something that usually starts out as a marvelously meaningful and romantic act turn into a barren forest or worse, a battleground? Sexual problems run the gamut from relatively minor (bad timing, boring, mediocre sex) to serious dysfunction. They range from one partner getting off and the other being continually left high and dry to more serious trouble, such as total incompatibility, impotence, or even a totally nonexistent sexual relationship.

There are as many reasons for this as there are pages in this book. Interestingly, of all the issues discussed within these pages, this one is equally attributable to women's and men's behavior. Whereas in some other areas we can point our fingers at our partner with a fairly clear conscience, in this instance we play an equal role in what goes down between us sexually. As always, let's begin by looking at his part.

WHY ARE THEY LIKE THIS?

I'm going to risk censorship here, adopt my Howard Stern voice, and put it just this bluntly: Men tend to think with their dicks. In less crude language, what this means is that *their libido often overwhelms their power of reasoning,* sometimes leading them to be sexual without necessarily being sensitive to our feelings and our needs. In all fairness, I've found that the older men get, the less tyrannized they are by their erections; I know a number of men in their forties who are relatively discerning about whom they are sexual with and often even turn sex down when it doesn't feel appropriate or right. But even they are fairly easily seduced. (Show them a sexy twenty-year-old and watch them turn into a high school senior within seconds.) So, fine. We get it. A man with an erection has a difficult time waiting, thinking about what he's doing, and being tuned in not only to his own emotions but also to his partner's.

Another difference (and this one isn't going to be any revelation to most of us) is that men are able to *compartmentalize* their sexuality, whereas our hearts and our sexual organs are *connected* by a thin silver thread. Again, rather than boring you with complicated psychological explanations, suffice it to say that a man's penis is external, whereas a woman's sexual organs are internal. Some "experts" have concluded that this explains why men are able to objectify their sexuality, whereas our inner emotions are all tied up with our feelings of sexual desire. Whether or not this is true, the result is that men tend to be able to have sex without love, while most women need to experience tenderness, affection, and warmth in order to be sexually receptive. This isn't true for every man and every woman. There are men who are exceptions and women who can and even prefer to be sexual without any emotional strings attached. But for the most part, men are more able and willing to be sexual even when intimacy is absent, while for most women, love is intimately connected to sex.

Our culture also reinforces men's objectification of the sexual act. Literally thousands of media images convey the message that women are sex objects meant to satisfy men's desires. Every car or vodka ad with a sexy woman as its focal point is directly targeted at promoting men's self-worth as contingent on sexual performance and women's worth as based on sexual allure.

Another equally compelling reason for men's seeming insensitivity to their partner's sexual needs has to do with the puritanical culture in which we were raised. Those of us who were brought up in the Judeo-Christian tradition received extremely contradictory and often mixed messages about women, who are portrayed as being either mothers or whores, martyrs or sinners. This accounts for the "I want a woman in the living room and a whore in the bedroom" mentality that many men bring to lovemaking. We can be lovely, modest, and discreet at a company dinner party yet let our slutty side rule when we trade our business suit for our favorite black thong. Poor babies! It must be horribly confusing.

Men may also use sex to compensate for areas of their lives or aspects of our relationship in which they feel weak or lacking. Remember, the same truth applies in bed and out of bed: *Men like to do what they do well.* Men who are confident of their sexual prowess are likely to seek sex, regardless of whatever else is going on in the relationship, because it's the one place where they feel confident and in charge. This explains one of the primary mysteries between men and women: Men will often turn to sex when a relationship is rocky, whereas sex is usually the last thing women want when they're not feeling close.

You'd think men would get the message when we pull away, but lovemaking seems to be the one area in which they act stupider than they do in any other part of their life. So is it sheer stupidity that makes men unaware of how to please their partner, often to the point of actually thinking she's satisfied when she's faked her fifteenth orgasm in a row?

I don't think so. Once again, I'm willing to give men the benefit of the doubt. Yes, many of them truly don't have a clue. They're operating in the dark and haven't the slightest idea how to stroke us, kiss us, and make us moan. But they want to, both because they genuinely love us and want to please us, and because their ego is on the line. That's okay. And we can make it easier for them, starting with looking honestly at our part in causing or creating sexual disharmony between our mate and ourselves.

HOW WE MAKE IT WORSE

Withholding sex is women's most typical way of exacerbating already existing problems in lovemaking. It's not that we mean to be bitchy or punishing. We simply are unwilling or unable to be sexual without feeling loved. Being sexual requires surrender, surrender requires trust, and anytime we feel mistrustful or alienated from our partner, we're unlikely to be open to his advances. We may indulge him, do it to get him off our back (or, rather, us off our back), put up with the sexual aerobics so that we can roll over and go to sleep. While it may sound as if we're being accommodating, we're actually being detached and increasing whatever estrangement exists. We may think we're in control, especially when he's happy, satiated, and seems to believe that everything's just peachy keen. But we know better, and what we know saddens us. Even if we're able to temporarily set aside our emotions and get into it, we still end up feeling empty, as if we've somehow compromised ourselves.

In addition, we're actually not doing our partner any favors. Letting him "have his way with us" or, to be crude, "servicing" him is akin to objectifying men, which is every bit as disrespectful as when they do the same to us.

We may also be victims of cultural conditioning that has given us negative and destructive messages regarding our sexuality. It's the old "good girls don't like sex" line, and not only is it outdated, it's also done an unimaginable amount of damage to women being able to create healthy and satisfying sexual relationships. Many of us were taught, some by our own mothers, that it was part of our "job description" to sexually satisfy our mate, whereas any sexual desire on our part meant that we were a whore or worse. Back when I was in high school, there were good girls and bad girls, and the distinction was simple: Good girls flirted and teased but drew the line at sex, whereas bad girls went all the way. Remember the "bad girl" with heavy eyeliner smoking in the school bathroom? We envied her, we gossiped about her, but we weren't about to be friends with her for fear of being labeled as "easy" or "promiscuous." A lot changes in twenty or thirty years, but despite the so-called sexual revolution, these messages are permanently ingrained in our psyche, which is why we may still have difficulty letting ourselves go.

In addition, it's common for women to use sexual favors as currency, trading "good behavior" for a roll in the sack. This isn't as manipulative or mechanistic as it sounds. Women have been doing it for centuries and understandably so. Withholding sex when our mate isn't good to us seems reasonable, since it's one of the best ways to get his attention. Rewarding him by initiating a sexy scene as positive reinforcement is equally effective.

But something about this bothers me. Recently, a friend of mine confided that she was seriously considering a divorce. After twenty years of marriage, her complaints included her husband neglecting her, refusing to support her career, never showing affection in public, yet insisting on sex every single night, after which he'd retire to the couch, saying it was the only way he could get a good night's sleep. Naturally this woman felt angry, disenchanted, and at her wits' end. But she had a last resort in mind: She'd decided to lock her bedroom door until her husband visibly shaped up. She felt this was a great plan, with a good chance of success. I felt more than a little troubled over her need to trade sex for love, and sad for all the women who came before us whose bodies were their only power and means of "currency."

Here's the problem: *When we withhold sex from our partner, we also deprive ourselves of one of life's most pleasurable experiences.* In speaking with thousands of women throughout the country, I'm convinced that my friend isn't in the minority. Many of us are either turned off or turning off our partner because we're angry and disappointed in the ways they haven't come through. It's a tricky trade-off, in some cases unavoidable, in that we can't—and shouldn't—force ourselves to be sexual when we don't feel safe. On the other hand, we deprive ourselves of the nurturing and nourishment that lovemaking provides. Some of us may feel so shut down that we don't even miss sex or notice that we and our partner have gone from being lovers to being roommates. But regardless of how much our libido has diminished, deep down we long to be touched, to be moved, to be carried away, if only for a few glorious moments.

WHAT HOOKS US

Knowing this, it may seem as if it would make sense for us to try to be more open to making love. But here's the hook: WE WANT TO FEEL LOVED. We may be horny as hell and our mate may be the greatest lover since Clark Gable, but if we don't feel loved, we struggle to open ourselves to sex. We need more pleasure in our lives; many of us feel touch deprived, and lovemaking can be a good way to break the impasse and create an opening to talk through problems in a softer, more loving way. Which leaves us with the challenge: Do we risk being sexual when everything doesn't feel just right in the hopes that making love will bring us closer to our partner? The following simple solutions will guide you through the ins and outs of improving your sexual relationship.

SIMPLE SOLUTIONS

Before we get into strategies, let's review our goal: to improve and enhance our sexual relationship with our mate. I remind you of this for two reasons. First, to encourage you to open yourself to sex even if doing so requires pushing through anger or forgiving your partner for ways in which you've been hurt. Second, to emphasize once more that these solutions, along with the rest offered in this book, are intended to make your life sweeter and more satisfying. In other words, especially in regard to sexuality, keep it uppermost in your mind that the point is to give yourself more of what you want, need, and deserve.

In this spirit, the first important strategy is to MAKE A CONCERTED EFFORT TO ALTER YOUR PERCEPTION OF LOVE-MAKING. For many women, sex has become a source of pressure, anxiety, and in the worst cases, a thankless task that we feel obligated to perform.

For this reason it's important to consider what you enjoy about making love. If sex is an okay but not necessarily wonderful part of your relationship, try to remember what it's been like at its best. What did your mate do that partic-ularly pleased you? What made the encounter particularly passionate or fulfilling? If your sex life has been fraught with ambivalence or something you force yourself to get through, then you'll have to reach further back in your memory to recall how lovely this experience can be.

Like romance, lovemaking is often at its peak at the begin-ning of a relationship. Not always, of course. Many sexual relationships deepen and intensify over time, as we become better, more experienced dance partners. But the beginning is often the most exciting, as we discover what it's like to kiss him, touch him, feel him inside us for the very first time.

Unless you're totally turned off (in which case, go on to the next chapter and come back to this when you're in the mood), remembering how luscious sex can be helps us to break through our inner barriers and consider the possibility of allowing more lovemaking in our lives.

Having a more positive attitude toward sex increases our availability. But we're not always available, nor should we be. The next important step is to know where we're at sexually and give our partner a strong and consistent message about our desires. Knowing where we're at is important because it enables us to make the right choice in any given situation. For example, if we're out of touch with ourselves and confused about whether we want to be lovers, we will either give up before we start or give our mate a mixed message, which will confuse and possibly anger him. But if we're clear, we can act on our desires.

For instance, you may be utterly disinterested in your partner's sexual advances after watching him flirt with another woman at a party the night before. You need to tell him his behavior was hurtful. Communicating your feelings can be enough to clear the air and to shift gears from anger to affection. Or let's say you want to be sexual but are truly too exhausted to make the effort (emphasis on the words *make the effort*). Your lack of interest has nothing to do with your mate, rather, you've been working eighty hours a week, taking care of two kids, and frankly, after setting the alarm for 6 A.M., you'd rather just curl up and go to sleep. In this case, the smart move is to tell your partner the truth—that you want to make love but you desperately need sleep, so how about a rain check? Or the roles may be reversed. You may be dying to jump his bones but are unsure as to whether or not he's interested. Ask! And, for god's sake, INITIATE. That's right. Women rarely make the first move, though if we did our partners would be thrilled, and we'd have both more control over lovemaking and more lovemaking in our lives. If anyone anytime in your life told you that "nice girls" don't act like they want it, they were giving you a bunch of crap. Wipe that thought out of your memory and go after what you want.

The point is, we can only say what we want if we know how we really feel. However, there are certainly times when our feelings are mixed, when we're somewhat interested but not all that motivated to initiate lovemaking or give our partner a clear sign to proceed. What do we do if we're ambivalent? It's easy. Go SLOWLY AND ONLY DO WHAT FEELS RIGHT. Don't feel pressured to go all the way if you're ready to stop at second base. It's perfectly fine to spend time in bed cuddling, kissing, and touching each other without every sexual encounter culminating in orgasm.

The next strategy has to do with that all-important factor in dealing with men: BE AWARE OF TIMING. Every male/female sexual relationship would improve immeasurably if both partners understood and respected the difference between the genders. For example, women consistently say that men go too fast and that they'd appreciate more foreplay. (Don't men ever read those magazine articles?) If they did, they'd know to slow down and do what it takes to get us ready. Men are equally predictable, especially in one particular way: For men, sex and talking about feelings (other than how good sex feels) are mutually exclusive. Translation? DON'T START A HEAVY CONVERSATION ABOUT YOUR RELATIONSHIP IN THE MIDDLE OF FOREPLAY. Assuredly he'll go limp, turn off faster than a lamp with a burnt-out bulb, and probably get mad that not only have you ruined any possibility of lovemaking, but you've also brought up his least favorite topic again. He may need to exercise patience in making love to you, but you need to be patient and refrain from initiating conversations about feelings when he's stroking your thigh.

The reason we do this is that when we feel his openness, we sometimes mistake it for an opening to talk about feelings rather than his expressing his excitement about getting into bed. So that you'll never be confused again: During sex, all he's thinking about is sex, and anything else is an unwelcome distraction. Author Robert Fulghum offers these five things not to say after turning off the light: (1) "Honey, I've decided to become a Baptist." (2) "I hate it when you touch me there." (3) "Please don't take this as criticism." (4) "I put a little dent in the Mercedes this morning." (5) "I want a divorce." Before or after sex (not right after!) bring up anything you want. Let lovemaking be its own language without introducing potential conflict into the mix.

Along the same lines, Don't Use Sex as a Weapon. It's powerful, and it often is effective, but this is one area in which I'd caution against "doing what works" in favor of taking the higher ground. Remember: There's a difference between saying no to sex because you're hurt, angry, or disinterested for any reason and withholding sex as a way to punish your mate. Remember the sixties slogan: Make love, not war. When we use sex as a weapon, to entice, intimidate, or threaten our mate, all love is lost in the transaction. Even if we temporarily feel like victors, we end up hurting both ourselves and the one we love.

However—and this is important—Don't Ever Do Anything in Bed That Feels Unsafe or Compromises Your Personal Integrity. In our effort to please or appease our mate, we may make love against our will, engage in sexual techniques that make us uncomfortable, or say something feels good when it doesn't, which is just another way of demonstrating low self-worth. Does faking orgasm fall into this category? Not necessarily. There are times when we choose to pretend, either to move the process along, get ourselves off the hook, or fake a fireworks display so that he'll relax and stop waiting for us to climax first. There's no right or wrong here, except for one caveat: Some women feel that faking an orgasm is tantamount to lying, which certainly compromises real intimacy, in which case, it's a bad idea. But if it works for you as an occasional tool you pull out of your bag of tricks, why not, especially if the end result is that both of you get what you want.

113

I've left this for last because it's the most important and, in some ways, the most challenging strategy in improving sexual relations. It's called show-and-tell, and it's the most important ingredient missing from intimate relationships. It's important because the only way your mate will learn how to please you is by watching how you please yourself and listening to you tell him what does it for you. The challenge is to get beyond our inhibitions so we will be able to be candid and vulnerable with our mate.

It pains me to imagine how many women lie in bed after sex feeling empty and ungratified when all they had to do was say "Over here, honey" or "Yes. That feels good" or "Look. This is how I do it." Words aren't even necessary. We can show our partner silently, in the dark, exactly where and how to touch us just right. We can encourage our partner to do the same. Some of the best advice I ever got was from a late-night talk show hostess who explained the simple fact that no one knows better than ourselves exactly what pleases us, therefore it only makes sense to let our partner in on the secret.

Enough said. Maybe it's time to put down this book and try something different tonight. P.S. Don't forget to compliment him. Men are suckers for compliments, especially in the sexual arena. Make sure he knows when he gets it right, because that way he'll do it again and again and again.

ON THE BRIGHT SIDE

More sex. Greater tenderness. Breaking through the barriers of past hurt and becoming closer and more intimate as a result of increasing and improving your lovemaking. I don't have to sell you on the pleasures of sex. Suffice it to say making love can be one of the sweetest, most creative aspects of our relationship. The more we cultivate it, the more we'll get out of it.

8

If he acts as if he deserves a medal for doing what you do twenty-four hours a day

Have you noticed that when men make the slightest effort, they boast, preen, and carry on as if they've climbed Mount Everest instead of having thrown in one load of laundry—*one*—as if you could even count the loads of laundry you've done in the past weeks, months, and years.

Now I know this is going to take some serious concentration, but think hard: When was the last time anyone thanked you for making dinner, driving the car pool, or folding the laundry? I could go on and on . . . As always, to be fair, plenty of men do plenty of chores without expecting a round of applause. But we're talking about the ones who don't.

More women than not profess to be involved with men who act as if they should be named "Man of the Year" on the cover of *Time* magazine any time they extend themselves. Janet illustrates this particular issue well in describing a recent episode in her relationship. She says, "Todd and I were having dinner at our friends' house. We were all sitting around the table when someone complimented the hostess, Claire, on her homemade lasagna, which was out of this world. Her husband, Peter, immediately piped up and reported that he'd grated the cheese (now that deserves a medal!), at which point Todd, not to be outdone, bragged about the fact that he'd made macaroni and cheese (Kraft's macaroni and cheese, to be exact) for the kids last Tuesday when I had a late-night meeting at work. He actually went on and on about how great it turned out and how the kids cleaned their plates, while Claire and I looked at each other, both annoyed and amused. I just don't get it. Todd and I both work full-time, and I make dinner every single night. Yet he acts like some kind of hero the one time he opens a box of macaroni and cheese, not to mention the fact that the dirty dishes were still in the sink when I dragged myself home exhausted at ten o'clock at night."

It's wonderful when our partners pitch in, but why do we have to reward and reinforce them for doing what we do as a matter of course? Why can't they just figure out what's needed and do it without being asked?

WHY ARE THEY LIKE THIS?

I hate to repeat the same lame yet valid explanation, but I'll have to: That's how they were brought up.

It may be maddening, but it's still true: Men who were excused from taking responsibility for parenting or doing domestic tasks actually believe that they're doing us a favor when they do anything outside of their prescribed roles. Not just excused but in many cases encouraged by mothers who labored thanklessly, by fathers who gave their sons both implicit and explicit messages that "real men don't do dishes," and by the culture at large in which, until quite recently, gender roles have been extremely well defined.

Personally, it thrills me to no end that my daughter is taking shop and my son is taking home economics classes at school. I don't know about you, but when I was thirteen, I was learning how to make Jell-O parfaits while my male schoolmates were building tables.

So men get a little break here. It's not entirely their fault that they've been raised to think that they're exempt from certain responsibilities, and then act like they're ace husbands, fathers, or helpmates when they do something outside their defined role. Of course, this doesn't make it any less annoying when we take on many responsibilities, day in and day out, without hearing "thank you," much less expecting a ticker tape parade.

Sixteen years ago, when our first child, Zoe, was born, I realized how at this point in history the majority of people in our society still appear shocked when men assume domestic responsibilities, whereas "women's work" is taken for granted. My ex-husband, Gary, was far more experienced at caring for newborns than I was. He'd worked in day care, whereas I'd never even baby-sat. Gary was totally involved in every aspect of caring for Zoe, including, of course, changing her diapers. I can still remember how furious I was whenever friends, strangers, or even my parents would carry on and on and on about what a marvelous father Gary was (and still is) when he would feed or burp or change our baby. But you can rest assured, no one noticed, much less complimented, me for doing the very same things.

Taking a step back, perhaps the same is true in reverse. I have to be honest and say that the first time I changed a tire, I called everyone I knew, starting with my boyfriend, to brag about my accomplishment. Whether it's having changed the oil or sanding the floor, I do seem to seek a pat on the back for undertaking tasks that men routinely perform without expecting any reward.

Having evened out the scales a bit, it's still frustrating when our partner needs constant reinforcement for doing what we do as a matter of course, twenty-four hours a day, 365 days a year, without expecting or receiving any kudos. But, as usual, we may be contributing to this problem in any or all of several ways.

HOW WE MAKE IT WORSE

When we want our mate to take more responsibility and he actually comes through, we may get so excited that we go off the deep end, thanking and rewarding him beyond what's necessary. Now don't misread me: Positive reinforcement is good. It gets results, which is our objective. What's tricky is to find the right balance between rewarding our mate so much or in such a way that he comes to expect it, and using positive reinforcement in a moderate and useful fashion. We have to be discerning about when and how to use positive reinforcement so that it serves, rather than sabotages, our goal, which is to stop rewarding our partner every time he does the right thing.

Another way we exacerbate this problem is by our not expecting to be rewarded (thanked, acknowledged, complimented) for our contributions. Some of this comes from having been taught that modesty is a virtue, that blowing our own horn is unbefitting and unladylike. What a crock! I wish every woman could have her own billboard with flashing neon lights listing every single task she performs on any given day. Once again, conditioning runs deep. Even when we intellectually know that we deserve appreciation, a little voice inside our head still says: "Classy women don't boast about their achievements." And believe me, it's just as much of an achievement to get three screaming kids to stop killing one another as it is to be there for our aging parents or negotiate a million-dollar contract for our company.

In short, we have to be a little more prudent in rewarding our mate and a lot more willing to bestow "medals" on ourselves for all we do. Why? Because the more appreciation we receive for our efforts, the less resentful we feel about having to constantly reinforce our partner, which naturally makes us mad.

WHAT HOOKS US

There's a good reason why we get mad at constantly rewarding our mate while receiving little or no appreciation in return. Here we are, lavishing praise on our partner, while *no one notices how hard we work and how much we do.* It's really not that big a deal to thank or compliment our mate; what gets us is how terribly unappreciated we feel.

Being taken for granted makes us feel angry, resentful, even invisible, which is the worst feeling of all. We feel like a nonperson, a commodity of sorts, which isn't acknowledged, yet without which our relationship and/or our family would most likely fall apart.

Once again (believe me, I'm getting as sick of saying this as you are of hearing it and we're only in chapter 8) it's up to you to actively alter the present situation by trying some of the following solutions.

SIMPLE SOLUTIONS

This one really is simple. GO AHEAD AND GIVE HIM A MEDAL. I'm serious, but don't you be. Make a joke out of it if you have to. The next time your partner makes a federal case over making the bed or going grocery shopping, hand him a plastic trophy or put a big gold star on his forehead. (Maybe I'll manufacture pins that say: "My Hero" and sell them on the home shopping network.) We can start having fun (or making fun) of how much positive reinforcement men need, but we need to feel appreciated in order to lighten up and stop resenting him.

There are two main ways to get appreciation: by GIVING OURSELVES A MEDAL and by ASKING OUR PARTNER TO CONSCIOUSLY ACKNOWLEDGE AND SHOW APPRECIATION FOR OUR EFFORTS.

Giving ourselves a medal isn't quite as easy as it sounds. What's required is giving ourselves credit for everything we do, which means taking the time to stop and write down every single way in which you expend effort, whether it's making a living, scrubbing the toilet, taking your kid (or your cat) to the doctor, lending a sympathetic ear when a friend is freaking out, or being loving toward your partner in countless unsolicited ways.

Go ahead and make your list. Include everything you

do. Now stop and ask yourself this question: "In what ways am I willing to reward myself?" After making her list, one woman I know immediately signed up for a weekend women's retreat. Another went out and bought herself the blouse she'd been coveting. And another chose to reward herself with a leisurely long-distance call to one of her closest friends, with whom she hadn't spoken for the past six months.

Rewarding ourselves is fairly simple once we get into the habit. Getting our *partner* to reward us takes a little more savvy. How can we get him to express appreciation without giving him elaborate instructions, which naturally diminishes, if not entirely destroys, our pleasure at having been acknowledged?

Here's the key: Remember, men love to do what they're good at, so GIVE HIM THE CHANCE TO SHINE. Your partner is far more likely to learn how to express appreciation if he feels confident of his ability to deliver. A few years ago, in the middle of a January blizzard in Minneapolis, I went to meet my friend Jill for coffee and inadvertently locked my keys in the car. I walked into the café, and asked the manager if he had a coat hanger so I could try to get the door open. Within seconds, seven men jumped out of their chairs, tripping over one another to go out in the thirty-below-zero windchill, eager to take on the challenge of getting into my car. I couldn't believe it! We can't get them to do the most trivial errand or household task, but they jump at the chance to be out in a blizzard twisting a mangled coat hanger, as if getting my car opened was an Olympic event. All I can figure is that it's an ego thing— a grown man's version of high school competitive sports.

The point is, if you approach your mate in the right spirit, preferably asking him to do something he's good at, he may surprise you by coming up with a few rewards that haven't occurred to you; he may even amaze you by offering to take some of the burden off your shoulders or suggest that you take a few days to go visit your sister in Florida.

Okay, that's the best-case scenario. But it's not out in left field. There's also the possibility that sharing your list or talking about your need for appreciation may make him angry or defensive. Prepare yourself for him to react with words such as "No one's making you do all that" or "Give me a break. Everyone should have it as good as you do." This is a lousy, unfair response, but for whatever it's worth, what he's really saying is: "I feel bad that you have to work so hard" or "I'm a rotten husband. Apparently I'm not being supportive and loving." If you find yourself in this position, you have two choices: You can stop the conversation and accept that he's not ready or willing to deal with your feelings. Or you can neutralize his feelings by reassuring him that you're fully aware of how hard he tries and then give him concrete ways he can show his appreciation.

If you decide to go for it, you have to be willing to be vulnerable. ASK, DON'T DEMAND. Express your need; don't berate him for past behavior. For instance, saying, "Are you totally blind or do you just not care that I'm so overworked I'm ready to drop" is guaranteed to provoke an argument. On the other hand, saying, "Honey, I'm so exhausted. I really need you to remind me that I'm doing a great job," gives him a way to be president of your fan club, which is what he truly wants to be.

Finally, BE A GOOD ROLE MODEL. Although, as we've discussed, it's important to be judicious in meting out rewards, show him how to express appreciation by continuing to praise his efforts. If he still doesn't get it, force the issue by explaining it in simple terms. After reinforcing him, say, "Doesn't it feel great to be appreciated? That's what I need from you." Hopefully, with time, the message will sink in.

He may never be as forthcoming with appreciation as you'd like, but notice any and all efforts in the right direction. If he totally blows it, here's a dramatic last resort: Go on temporary strike. Think picket lines and union workers demanding appropriate compensation for their work. If you've tried everything and he still takes you for granted, *stop doing so much.* Sometimes doing less is the only way to get men to wake up and notice how much we normally take on. If you try this option—for instance, not making dinner for a few nights, letting the laundry pile up, or acknowledging his birthday with a Hallmark card instead of a lavish gift and a homemade chocolate cake—it won't take long for him to notice what's missing in his life. This isn't punishment, although he will probably accuse you of just that. Rather it's a way of taking care of *yourself,* which is the real point of this book. One cautionary note: Be casual. Don't turn this into warfare; simply give yourself a little vacation from some of your responsibilities, which may both force your mate to show more appreciation as well as provide the added benefit of reducing your stress.

ON THE BRIGHT SIDE

Giving your mate a medal may make him laugh and get him to see that it's ludicrous to expect applause anytime he performs well. Giving yourself medals, on the other hand, is an important way of acknowledging yourself for how hard you work and how much you do. The more you appreciate yourself, the more likely your partner is to notice, especially when you bring home a bouquet of fresh flowers you've bought yourself to celebrate finishing a long and arduous project at work.

Sometimes men are just plain oblivious. It actually doesn't occur to them to make overt gestures of appreciation. Give him a few clues, and you might be surprised at what a quick learner he is. Either way, anything you do to reward yourself is well deserved. Keep up the good work.

9

If he accuses you of being high-maintenance

Here we go again. High-maintenance—another one of those vague, male buzzword insults that mean nothing in particular but has the power to make us think there's something seriously wrong with us. Clearly, being labeled "high-maintenance" is meant as a criticism, which definitely goes in the debit column of our partner's romantic checkbook.

Years ago, when I first heard this term, I assumed it referred to extremely wealthy, spoiled women who expected to be waited on hand and foot at the snap of their fingers. You know who I mean: Imelda Marcos with her eighty thousand pairs of shoes (after ten thousand, who's counting?); Leona Helmsley, who apparently wasn't satisfied living for free in one of New York's finest hotels; Ivana Trump demanding caviar, a Mercedes-Benz, and diamonds from Tiffany's. I probably wasn't being fair, stereotyping these women according to their social status, when for all I know they're as gracious and unassuming as can be.

I didn't, however, realize how broadly and loosely this term is being applied to women, including myself. Apparently being high-maintenance means everything from having six different shades of nail polish to sending back bad food at restaurants, to hiring a kid to shovel the driveway, to insisting on respect in the workplace, to expecting our partner to have a simple, straightforward conversation about our relationship when, god forbid, he isn't in the mood.

In short, being high-maintenance apparently describes any woman who has the nerve to *know what she wants and who believes she deserves to get it*—or at least is willing to try. I've been called high-maintenance so many times I'm beginning to feel like a car. Initially I laughed it off, considering it a backhanded compliment. After all, better to be perceived as strong and assertive than as a submissive groveler, grateful for any crumbs that fall our way. Then I started to resent it as an unfair and undeserving characterization that enables men to justify their feelings of pressure and excuses their unwillingness to give what's asked of them.

In truth, I expect a lot. I'm extremely clear about what I want and quite determined to get it. For example, I can walk into a clothing store and pick the perfect outfit off the racks, pay for it, and be out the door in a record eleven minutes. I've been known to return closed mussels, I expect phone calls to be returned within a reasonable time frame and lovers to pay quality attention when we're together. None of which I apologize for. I'm also generous, compliant, accommodating, and conciliatory, even when the situation calls for a little bitchiness on my part. I give at least as much as I ask for, which seems to be at the root of the problem.

In doing research for this chapter, I asked each of my ex-husbands and my most recent ex-lover to tell me honestly if they thought of me as high-maintenance. Each said yes without a second's hesitation. So I pushed for a definition, asking, "What exactly makes you see me this way?"

One said, "You expect people to do nice things for you." (Now, that's a crime!) Another said, "You ask a lot from the people in your life." The third said, "You demand a high level of honesty and intimacy, which frankly makes me feel pressured." If we combine their responses into a single sentence, it would be: You give a lot and you expect a lot, which apparently is more than some men can handle.

The fact that the label "high-maintenance" has become another one of men's worst insults is both interesting and disturbing. One would think that as we approach the millennium, more and more men would be looking for smart, stimulating, confident women who can hold their own or even give them a run for their money. But no.

As we've explored earlier in this book, there's a distinction between *serving* our partner and being *subservient*. It's fun to occasionally be demure or deferential, but ultimately we want real men who can handle real women with all the trimmings. So why can't they deal with this powerful a package? What threatens men about women who know what they want and know how to get it?

WHY ARE THEY LIKE THIS?

Men translate high-maintenance as: She wants something from me and I don't have it to give. *Plainly, they feel pressured.* Another important insight about men is that most of the time they think we're asking for much more than we really are. For example, when we say we'd like more attention, they hear, "I have to stop everything else I'm doing and spend all my time with her." Or when we mention that it would be nice to take a vacation together, he gets freaked out that we're expecting a month in Monaco, when we'd be perfectly delighted to go camping for the weekend.

Our partner also may interpret our desires—and our willingness to pursue them—as a covert message that he should be giving us what we want. But it isn't true. Just because we have a standing pedicure appointment doesn't mean that we expect him to buy us new sandals to show off our perfectly polished lavender toes. Remember: Men want to please. When they feel insecure about their capacity to provide what we want, they often go on the offensive, criticizing us for "making" them feel inadequate and insecure.

Second, *even men who are relatively secure with a strong woman may struggle to reconcile the seeming contradiction between femininity and assertiveness.* Men say they want powerful women, but watch what happens when the real thing shows up. Recently my friend Nancy, who is the vice president of advertising for a large department store in Portland, met a man she really liked. He was attractive, successful, and, best of all, he actively pursued the relationship, wining and dining her, making plans and making noise about getting more involved. But on their third date Nancy apparently blew it. She, her date, and his two best friends were out having a drink. His best friend suggested they go to a karaoke bar; Nancy made the cardinal mistake of saying, "You know, I really don't like karaoke." That's all she said. Four days went by, and she didn't hear from this man. When she called to ask what was going on, he informed her that he'd been appalled at her rudeness. Why couldn't she just have gone along with what everyone else wanted to do? Understand, she didn't say, "Only losers like karaoke." She didn't refuse to go. She merely expressed her preference, which was enough to send this man running away as fast as he could. After admiring her confidence and assertiveness, it turned out that what he wanted was a submissive woman who'd let him call the shots.

The third reason men shy away from "high-maintenance" women is that *they're scared that they'll have to give back more than they care to.* Again, they're mistaken, but try convincing them of that. The truth is that just because we make a big surprise party for his birthday doesn't mean we expect anything more than a carefully chosen card and maybe a small, thoughtful gift for ours. We've been over this already, but I'll say it again: Women give because we want to give, not because we're looking for exact reciprocity. Yes, we want our gestures acknowledged and appreciated. No, we don't expect our partner to respond in kind.

But he *thinks* we do, which is why the more we give, and the more he interprets our generosity as a blatant or subtle message of what we expect in return, the more he accuses us of being high-maintenance. This is unfair and seems a bit crazy. Here we are, going out of our way, and we get stomped on for being generous. This happened when I was planning my second wedding. I wanted to serve a catered Caribbean buffet, but Joey kept saying, "It's fine to just have beer and pretzels." It wasn't fine with me, especially since I was shelling out the dough (which I was perfectly fine with). But instead of appreciating my ability to throw a beautiful wedding, he kept harping on the cost, partly because he really was okay with pretzels and beer, and possibly because he felt uncomfortable that he couldn't pay his share. I tried explaining that I wanted to do this, that I could afford it, but nothing I said made a difference. Even at our wedding, at which everyone was oohing and aahing over the fabulous food, he still never swallowed his pride and allowed that we'd made the right choice.

If this sounds like a no-win situation, hang on. Before we explore simple solutions, let's take an honest look at how we may worsen the situation in some of the following ways.

HOW WE MAKE IT WORSE

There are three distinct ways in which we may unintentionally contribute to this problem. First, by being overly demanding. This has more to do with communication than with what we're actually asking for. Again, the key word is *ask*. There's a real difference between saying "Honey, could you please get me my bathrobe" and "I need my bathrobe," which comes across as a demand. Men—well, all of us, for that matter—are much more accommodating when asked for a favor rather than issued a command. It's about being courteous. We needn't alter our desires or expectations; we just need to frame them in a more appealing fashion. For example, instead of berating a waiter for the food being cold, it's just as easy—and much nicer—to politely ask him to heat it up. Likewise, if you want to have an intimate conversation with your partner, don't come on like gangbusters, insisting he drop everything and talk to you right this minute! Use discretion and be gracious at all times. *Being gracious doesn't mean being fake or ingratiating; it means being a "lady" in the best sense of the word.*

We may also reinforce our mate's perception that we're high-maintenance by using threats, shaming him, or provoking jealousy to get what we want. For instance, one woman may give her partner the message that if he doesn't straighten up and start being more ambitious, she just may look elsewhere for someone who can play at her level. Another woman may shame her husband by talking about all the material things she wants but unfortunately can't have, given his modest paycheck. Yet another woman may play the game of making her partner jealous by talking about other men who are more successful, emotionally available, or able to provide some of the things she wants and isn't getting from her mate.

This is a dangerous and destructive game. Remember: *Men have fragile egos!* Our egos aren't nearly as fragile as theirs, maybe because their lives revolve mostly around themselves whereas we are consistently aware of and involved with others—our children, friends, aging parents, and other loved ones whom we care about and take into consideration. It's a well-kept secret (which we all harbor) that women are fundamentally stronger than men, which means we can afford to indulge our partner's ego when we need to without letting him off the hook or subjugating our desires.

Then again, there's also the possibility that we really *are* high-maintenance in a way that turns our partner off. Some women are overly demanding as a result of having felt deprived or neglected in the past. We may be making up for lost time, trying to remedy past wounds by wanting more than we truly need in order to be happy.

This is worth examining. I know I've been guilty of this behavior. The degree of criticism and lack of affirmation in my childhood definitely resulted in my having a certain urgency, even desperation, that translates into needing a great deal of approval from others. I'm still learning how to moderate my hunger, be it for new clothes, attention from men, or approval from editors. My therapist's last words of wisdom before I finished therapy with him were, "Watch your appetite." He didn't mean go on a diet; he meant be aware of how you compensate for what was missing in your childhood by frantically seeking love, in whatever form, as an adult. I've thought about his advice a lot, and I've heeded it. When I feel compelled to shop when my account is overdrawn or call an ex-boyfriend who's repeatedly hurt me, I know it's time to stop and face my feelings of emptiness without doing anything stupid or self-destructive.

I'm not telling you to settle for less than what you truly want. But it is instructive to understand how and why we may act in ways that our partner describes as high-maintenance.

WHAT HOOKS US

Naturally we get riled at being called "high-maintenance." We interpret it as meaning, "You're just too much to deal with," which none of us wants to hear. We feel defensive, even ashamed, at wanting or expecting what we actually think we deserve. Our knee-jerk response is to bolster our diminished self-esteem by reminding our partner of all the times we put our own needs aside or list all the ways in which we are easy to live with.

We don't have to defend ourselves! In fact, we can be proud of being high-maintenance, especially if we redefine the term in a more positive light, which is the first simple solution.

SIMPLE SOLUTIONS

High-maintenance women unite! It's time to stand up for our rights. Our right to speak up and say what's on our minds. Our right to pursue pleasure and enjoyment, whether it's shopping, sailing, or a weekend at a spa with our best friend, as long as we can afford it and have a clear understanding with our mate. WE HAVE THE RIGHT TO ASK FOR WHAT WE WANT, even if those around us are being wishy-washy or feeling intimidated by our decisiveness. In other words, let's redefine *high-maintenance* as strength rather than superiority.

With this new attitude comes the responsibility of communicating our desires in a way that works. Remember: no demands. Replace the words "I expect" or "Gimme" with "I'd like," "I want," or "Would you mind doing me a favor?" Saying "thank you" is especially important, in that it expresses our appreciation and gratitude, neutralizing our partner's perception of us as being overly demanding.

On a strategic level, be sure to LET YOUR PARTNER KNOW THAT HE'S GOOD ENOUGH, giving enough, and doing fine at satisfying your needs. (Fudge if you need to.) If you want something that he can't provide, either keep it to yourself or figure out a way to get it yourself, but no matter what, don't make him feel ashamed of what he can realistically give. This doesn't mean you shouldn't ask for what you want. One of the fun parts of a relationship is doing nice things for each other, but it stops being fun when one or the other of us feels put upon. For example, asking your husband to run to the supermarket at 1 A.M. because you have a sudden craving for Ben & Jerry's Cherry Garcia ice cream is not okay unless you're pregnant, in which case nothing is too much to ask. You can be sensitive to your mate's feelings without seriously compromising your right to ask for what you want.

ON THE BRIGHT SIDE

Being high-maintenance has a slew of tangible rewards. If we have high expectations, we usually get a lot in return. If we have mediocre expectations, we often end up settling or getting less than what we really want.

Having our partner see us as high-maintenance can also yield certain surprising rewards. Even if he's intimidated, he may respect our tenacity and level of self-esteem. He may shoot higher, which can improve his self-image and even the playing field. Our relationship can also benefit from finding the right balance between our overly high standards and his hesitation or restraint. The best-case scenario is one in which we accept and appreciate the differences, using them to strengthen our relationship.

10

If he isn't supportive of or involved in your career, interests, or hobbies

———◆———

The following conversation was overheard at a sidewalk café:

WOMAN 1: So Jack and I were having dinner at Nancy's.

WOMAN 2: Wait . . . did you get the promotion?

WOMAN 1: I'm about to tell you. So we were in the middle of dinner when Jack starts telling everyone about how he's this close to signing the contract with this big distributor he's been pursuing for months. In the middle of his talking about it, Nancy asks me if I got the promotion. . . .

WOMAN 2: You got it, right?

WOMAN 1: Right. *(The two women clink cups of cappuccino)* So I start talking about how excited I am

and how they put out this memo at work and everything, and how I'm going to get a big raise and get
to go to the annual convention in New York. Nick
and Nancy congratulate me, and then Jack opens his
big mouth and says, "Yeah, and then that asshole
boss of yours will work you harder than ever. You
know, that guy is a real jerk. You probably got the
promotion because he knows he can manipulate you
and get another twenty hours of work out of you."

Ouch! There are a couple of possible interpretations of
Jack's seemingly mean and insensitive remark, but only
one is even remotely positive, and it's the following response: "I feel protective of my wife so I'm dissing her
boss (her career and her promotion) because I care about
her so much."

I'm willing to buy this, if for no other reason than I'm
a sucker for men who express their love by taking on the
role of protector and defender. You have to agree, it's
sweet and it's wonderful to know that our partner takes
it personally when we're threatened or potentially in dan-
ger. (I once fell in love with a man I'd known less than
an hour when he got in the face of a guy in a bar who
was bugging me and said, "You say one more word to my
girlfriend and I'll smack you so hard you won't remember
your name"—and I hate violence!) Who can resist a man
who comes to the rescue—a version of the knight in shin-
ing armor that's fast becoming extinct.

Having complimented men for their protective instinct, it
still hurts when our mate is unsupportive, disinterested, or
downright dismissive about our careers or other meaningful
aspects of our lives. Back to the conversation at the café.

Jack, Woman 1's husband, had the right intentions, but his delivery totally missed the mark. Another example of men's cluelessness: Here's his wife, celebrating her promotion, and what does he do? He knocks the wind out of her sails, when there were so many other wonderful ways he could have responded.

Hey, Jack, try: "Barb (let's give her a name) worked so hard to get the promotion!" Or "I'm so proud of you, babe," or, for that matter, he could have just kept his mouth shut and not said anything at all. What Barb—and most of us—want is for our partners to support our endeavors, celebrate our achievements, and share in whatever interests and engages us.

Unfortunately, many men fall short in this department. Although career is the area in which this is most prevalent, numerous women complain that their partner is unsupportive and uninvolved in other significant ways. For example, Paula, an office manager for a large furniture wholesaler, says that her husband, George, "gives me a play by play about what's happened at work every day, but when I start telling him about my day at the office, he gets that glazed look in his eyes, and within a few minutes, changes the subject or starts clearing the table." (At least George clears the table!)

Why do men go into a self-imposed coma when their partners are right in the middle of sharing important information? I would be tempted to attribute this particular behavior to their being threatened by women's success in the workplace, except for the fact that this dynamic extends into numerous different aspects of male-female relationships.

For example, when Susan and Tom had their first baby, they agreed that she would quit her job and stay home with their son, while Tom would support them financially.

Susan's complaint: "No matter how tired I am from taking care of a two-month-old baby all day long, I always make sure to ask Tom about what's going on at work. When I first had the baby, I used to tell him everything that Jake had done that day, but after a while it was obvious he could care less about how breast-feeding went or how long Jake slept or even the fact that he'd smiled for the first time. So I stopped sharing all this stuff, knowing I was boring him, and just waited to see if he'd ask. Needless to say, he doesn't. I still tell him anything unusual or amazing that's happened, but I've pretty much accepted that he's bored by the details of being a mom, which is really upsetting, since I'm totally devoted to raising our child. You'd think he'd want to know everything about his son."

You'd think. In fact, we wish. We desperately wish that our partners cared about and asked about and were extremely involved and supportive of what truly matters to us, whether it's our career, being a mother, or finally taking a painting class that we've been talking about for years. My friend Vicky describes her husband, Bruce, as being "indifferent" to her joining a health club and religiously working out three times a week. "I'm serious," she says. "Bruce knows I've been trying for years to get in shape, he knows how hard it is to drag myself to the gym. I've already lost seven pounds and two inches, and when I come home sweating, and tell him I'm up to twenty-five minutes on the StairMaster, he doesn't say anything." "C'mon, he must say something," I reply. "No, really." Vicky pauses, gets a pained expression on her face, and then recalls, "Oh, right, a few nights ago he said, 'You really ought to take a shower, honey,' as if I was going to get in bed with him with sweat dripping down my arms."

Rachel, a feature editor at a big city newspaper, similarly

relates, "Recently I realized that I've been so stressed out that I had to do something about it. So I started taking a Zen meditation class, and now I meditate twice a day. I'm really excited about what I'm doing, but the few times I've tried to explain to my boyfriend, Ethan, how meditating has changed my life, he just says 'Uh-huh' or changes the subject. It makes me question whether or not he's the right person for me to be involved with." Rachel neither wants nor expects Ethan to get up at 5 A.M. and contort his limbs into the lotus position; she simply wants him to understand and support her doing something that she's so excited about.

Is this too much to expect? Apparently. Of course, as in all areas of relationship dynamics, the seriousness of this problem varies from woman to woman. It's one thing for our partner to be less enthusiastic about our career or other interests than we'd like, but it's another thing for him to be somewhat detached, and it's utterly unacceptable when our mates dismiss, criticize, or worst of all, degrade the very things that are most meaningful in our lives. Lots of men just don't seem to have the skills (thoughtfulness, courtesy, wherewithal) to pay attention to what matters to us. We want to share the daily details of our lives, and we want him to want to know anything and everything that makes our hearts sing.

Now this definitely may be asking too much. For example, I love reading. I'm constantly giving books to other people, marking incredibly well-written passages, and even reading them over the phone. Naturally, I kept giving my favorite books to my last boyfriend, hoping he'd be as moved, excited, and passionate as I was. It took a while for me to "get it," but after finding the sixth unopened one beside his bed, I finally stopped showing up with books, handing them to him in the hopes that he'd read them. I even tried finding books related to his interests, one on trees, another on Native American rituals, which he claimed to be extremely interested in. Those books, too, are still sitting unopened on his coffee table. The guy just isn't into reading, that's all there is to it.

That's one level of uninvolvement, and it's relatively innocuous. No two people, whether they're friends, lovers, or lifelong partners, are going to share the exact same interests. But whether one loves reggae music and the other is fascinated by deep-sea diving, loving someone requires making an effort to support and understand what gives their lives purpose, meaning, or maybe, just a paycheck. Some men simply need to be reminded to be more involved and responsive, which we'll talk about in a moment. But first, what about the guy who treats his wife as if her career is secondary, who is critical of her friends or hobbies, or who belittles her for taking belly-dancing classes or joining a study group at church? It's time to look at why men act this way, and the reasons better be good, because even I can hardly bear to have to find "good" explanations to justify behavior that, frankly, seems inexcusable and unnecessary.

WHY ARE THEY LIKE THIS?

Let's start with the most obvious reason why men may not be supportive and involved in any number of important aspects of our lives: *They're threatened.* There, I said it. And trust me, they don't like hearing this. Every time I've raised this possibility to a man in my life or to one of my clients, they insist it isn't so. It doesn't matter how it's phrased. I've tried mentioning it casually (Is there anything about my work that makes you feel a little weird?). I've tried explaining it nicely ("I think you might be a little threatened by how much money I make, how many friends I have, how many . . ."). I've even tried direct confrontation ("Ron, it sounds as if you might feel a little threatened by Mimi's getting elected as treasurer of the school board"), and still an adamant "No!"

Fine. Men might not be able to acknowledge the ways in which our career or other involvements are threatening, but that won't keep us from examining this as a reasonable underlying motivation for their behavior. First, let's define *threatened.* I'm using this term to describe any way in which our partner responds to our interests in a way that makes him feel scared, vulnerable, or as if his ego, power, or masculinity is at risk. In simpler terms, if we're prospering in our career and his is limping along, he may feel impotent or defensive about his performance as a breadwinner. If his social life is slim to nil and we have a million friends, the contrast may evoke feelings of being insecure and unpopular, no matter how many times he swears up and down that he'd rather sit home alone than hang out with your friends, who bore him to tears. If he's getting a beer belly and we're getting whistled at, he may be secretly afraid that, unless he gets off the couch and stops snarfing down donuts, he may lose us to a younger, sexier competitor. We're talking male ego here, and I don't care how far we've come in the feminist movement, contemporary male egos are still fragile, which doesn't mean we have to cater to them; it's just smart to accept the fact that in this sense, we really haven't come that far.

If he denies these feelings, this doesn't mean he's lying. The majority of men are either unaware or incapable of acknowledging that they feel threatened. Maintaining an image (first to themselves, then to the rest of the world) has been so drummed into them that they might not even experience the feeling of fear, much less have the words and/or the courage to express it. Back to the primal, cave-man metaphor: The men we're in love with come from a long line of ancestors for whom expressing fear in the face of spear-yielding enemies was literally a matter of life and death. Again, this conditioning extends as a primal imprint into contemporary times, even when the "enemy" has been reduced to the guy who's trying to cut in front of them in traffic or "their woman" raising insecurities about their strength and masculinity.

So if they're threatened, why don't they get their act together instead of putting us down? Good question. In the best of all possible worlds, our achievements would motivate and inspire our mate to rise to the occasion by getting more serious about his life, his health, his relation-ships, and any other ways in which he feels threatened by our success. I do know one man who, when his wife de-cided to go on a healthy macrobiotic diet, was so im-pressed by her energy and slimmed down figure that he followed suit, but he's the exception. More often men deal with feeling threatened by feeling sorry for themselves or taking it out on their girlfriend, lover, or wife.

A second explanation (not excuse!) is that *men are com-petitive by nature and therefore see our success as a chal-lenge or threat.* You may play into this (we'll explore this possibility in the next section), but it's more likely that your partner is creating competition, especially if both of you are deeply committed to fast-track careers. When this happens, we become adversaries instead of allies, which is a real shame, since both our incomes are needed to make ends meet, and both of us are working hard enough, often within a highly stressful and competitive environment, without arguing over who is working harder.

Men also may genuinely feel upset about some aspect of our lives, most typically related to work. This is one of those "can't win for losing" sort of deals. He may feel badly that we have to work and wish that he could fully support us so that we could stay home with our kids or just have a more relaxed, leisurely existence. Or he may feel the opposite—angry that we don't have to work—and may resent that we get to sleep in, hang out at the mall, or just relax while he's knocking himself out making a living. What's a girl to do? Even if we reassure our mate that it's perfectly okay for us to have a career, he may still feel guilty that he can't provide in the way that he saw his father do, or even worse, sees his friends able to do. And if we aren't working outside the home, why should we have to apologize or defend how we spend our time? We don't. But we can be aware that our partner may be jealous or resentful of the fact that our life seems easier and more carefree than his does, which can account for his seeming lack of interest or outright denigration of our activities.

He may also feel left out. Men are weird in this way. You ask him to stop by at your office so that everyone can meet him, and he says he's too busy. You beg him to join you at your son's school conference, and he tells you to handle it and report back to you. Or you invite him to come to your Adult Children of Alcoholics group, and he refuses, saying he'd feel uncomfortable and out of place. Do they need a hand-delivered, engraved invitation to believe that they're truly welcome, that we want them, more than anything, to be a central part of our lives?

No, *what they need is to grow up.* They need to get over their insecurity that they won't fit in, they need to get beyond their narcissistic belief that they are the center of the universe, and they need to stop indulging themselves with self-pity and start giving us the support and encouragement we give them. That's assuming that we're treating our mate in the way we want to be treated.

HOW WE MAKE IT WORSE

We may unintentionally sabotage ourselves and feed into our partner's lack of support by going to one extreme or the other. In intimate relationships, women often make the mistake of either giving too much in order to get love and approval (it doesn't work!) or pulling back and withdrawing our support because we're sick and tired of giving so much. (Notice this is a vicious cycle; having gotten ourselves into this thankless position, we now have to get ourselves out.)

Here's how this pattern develops, starting with what makes us give too much or downplay our achievements so as to bolster our partner's confidence and ego. For example, let's say we know our partner is sensitive about the fact that our career is taking off while his is at a standstill. We spend hours helping him strategize ways to impress his boss while making sure not to mention that our manager took us out to lunch to compliment us on what a terrific job we're doing. He even hinted at a promotion. Or let's say we're miserable at work and thinking about quitting and looking for another job. Our boss is a tyrant, we've been passed up twice for a promotion, and everyone in the office is paranoid about getting laid off. It would help to be able to unburden ourselves to our partner, but knowing how tight money is—we just had to take another credit card advance—we keep our mouths shut, all the while praising him for working so hard and reassuring him that things will get better, even going so far as to offer to take on a second, part-time job.

The same tendency to suppress our own need for support and encouragement in order to prop up our partner extends beyond our careers. For example, we faithfully sit in the bleachers every Thursday night, cheering him on at his weekly softball game, but are hesitant to ask him to be at the bookstore poetry reading next Monday night at which, despite our terror, we've finally decided to stand up and read our first poem. Or we praise him for showing up at our daughter's dance recital. We've driven her to dance classes twice a week for the past six months and spent days sewing sequins on her tutu. But do we show our mate the incredibly dear note our daughter wrote us that afternoon, ending "Thanks for always being there for me, Mom"? No. We stuff it in our purse so he won't see it and feel slighted.

See the pattern? It almost goes without saying (but I'm going to say it just to be sure there's no misunderstanding) that there's nothing wrong with our being sensitive to our partner's feelings. Obviously, no matter how excited we are, bragging about being named employee of the month is just plain rude if our mate has just lost his job. Sharing our daughter's love note can wait until later, especially if her dad has cancelled an important meeting to be at her recital. That's just plain common sense. But when we repeatedly bridle our enthusiasm or refrain from sharing our accomplishments, we in fact give our mate the message that his feelings and concerns take precedence over ours. Every time we downplay our achievements, make light of what matters to us, or tiptoe around him so that he isn't threatened by our success, we reinforce that it's okay for him to ignore, dismiss, or diminish what's significant and meaningful in our lives.

Now, let's turn this upside down. A second, equally significant, way in which we may unwittingly collude in our partner's behavior is by going to the other extreme: giving him a taste of his own medicine, even though we may do it for entirely different reasons. We may be critical or unsupportive of our partner's career and other interests because we're angry or resentful at how we've been treated. Fair enough. No matter how loving we are, no one can give indefinitely without getting something back in return. We're human, which means that we react. If our partner is consistently negative about our career, after a while we're bound to be less supportive of his. If he constantly criticizes our best friend or is patronizing about our aerobics class (Beth, one of my clients, fled Friday-night dinner at her parents' when her husband, Peter, made a joke about middle-aged women looking like idiots jiggling up and down in their fancy sweatsuits), it's inevitable that we're going to start making digs about his best friend's drinking problem, or mention the cute guy in our aerobics class. Both extremes are understandable, but neither is useful. Whether we put ourselves down to build our partner up, or put him down because we're angry and hurt—doing so doesn't serve us, our relationship, or in any way help to resolve the problem. Playing down our accomplishments gives our partner tacit permission to do the same, and treating him as he treats us only reinforces bad behavior. Yes, he may get the point, but at what price? We end up sinking to his level, and except in the rarest of cases, he's more likely to retaliate than reciprocate, once again making us adversaries instead of allies.

Which brings us to the issue of competition. We've talked about men withholding support and encouragement because they feel competitive, but many women are guilty of the same offense. Another way in which we may be complicit in this behavioral pattern is by being competitive, especially in regard to our career. The problem then becomes a power struggle. For example, we may covertly or overtly play one-upmanship, either by boasting about how much money we're making, monopolizing the conversation with play-by-play details about work, or pushing him to be more savvy, aggressive, or ambitious on the job—after all, it's working for us. We may inundate him with stories about the drama and tension we experience in the workplace or complain about being overworked and stressed to the max. This is a form of: Who has it harder, you or me?

Being competitive is guaranteed to put our partner on the defensive. It's a losing strategy, one we resort to as a way to goad him into paying attention to our lives. Another way we do this is by shaming him: "I wouldn't have to work so hard if you had the balls to ask your boss for a raise." (I know you probably haven't ever said these words, but I bet you've thought them.) Or by complaining about how much we resent working or how stressful our lives are, which gives him the perfect opening to say something like, "How many times have I told you to look for a better job?" Or "So it's my fault that you have a miserable life" instead of what we want to hear, which is: "Honey, I'm sorry you're having a hard time. How can I help?" That's what we want. That's what we need. And not getting this basic support and encouragement is the source of our underlying hurt and resentment.

WHAT HOOKS US

All we really want is for our partner to "get" who we really are. That's the emotional bottom line. To be more specific, we want him to make the effort to understand our priorities, value how we spend our energy, recognize what's important to us, and, above all else, honor and respect who we really are.

The desire to be understood, to be loved and supported in the ways that we spend our energy, our time, our lives, is one of the unique qualities women bring to intimate relationships. This is so elementary that you'd think he'd not only want the same but would be ready, willing, and able.

He *isn't*. Or he *can't*. Or he doesn't want and need the same things we do, or at least, not to the same degree. Therein lies the problem. We interpret our mate's lack of involvement as lack of commitment, that is, if he really cared about me, he'd . . .

But love and level of commitment don't even enter into this equation. Men, in general, simply don't desire or require the same level of personal support and involvement that women crave. I know this is hard to swallow, but he doesn't necessarily care whether or not we're "into" his career. He may like that we show up at his soccer game, but if we didn't, it wouldn't particularly bother him. In short, this is another way in which men operate more independently than women. The problem is: He fails to come through because he bases what he gives on what he needs in a similar situation, rather than recognizing and responding to our needs, even though they're different from his.

This is human nature. Our tendency to love another person in the manner that we want to be loved is one of the biggest problems in intimate relationships. I know I've done it—I want to be cared for when I'm sick, so I drive over with chicken soup for my boyfriend when he's under the weather, knowing full well that he'd rather be alone. Or I offer to help him draft a work proposal when he clearly doesn't want my help, because I'd love for him to be willing to read and edit my writing.

But this strategy backfires more often than it succeeds. Instead of our mate mimicking our behavior, he's far more likely to feel pressured to be someone other than he is, which ultimately makes him feel that we don't "get" and accept who he is, anymore than he "gets" and accepts who we are. That's how couples get stuck. But there's a way out of this dilemma. So what can we do to encourage our mate to support us in such a way that convinces us he truly understand and respects who we are?

SIMPLE SOLUTIONS

First and foremost, we have to TAKE PRIDE IN OUR ENDEAVORS, regardless of our partner's response. It would be wonderful if he was extremely involved in our career, if he asked questions about how we handled our three-year-old's tantrum at the grocery store, if he listened raptly to what went on at our weekly support group, if he was sympathetic to our fight with our mother and offered to intervene, if he was so enthusiastic about our interest in bonsais that he agreed to cancel his weekly bridge game and take a class together at the local museum. Our mate may surprise us by doing any of the above, but pushing him is a turnoff, whereas asking is our only chance of getting more of what we want.

Why should we have to ask? Here we go again. He doesn't have to ask us to pay attention to what matters to him, so why should we have to express our desires (which are reasonable) as a formal request?

Because it works. At the risk of repeating myself, here's the short version: If you want him to be more involved in your career, Ask for His Support. How? First the "don'ts." Don't say: "I've been working at the agency for twelve years and you still haven't even seen my office." Rather, invite him for lunch and give him a tour. Introduce him to your coworkers and show him around the place, making sure to thank him for taking the time to show an interest in your career. Likewise, if you want him to share your newfound interest in gardening, invite him to accompany you to the nursery to help pick out seeds and ask him to help you plant tomatoes and cucumbers.

Men like to help. I can't emphasize this enough. If this flies in the face of your personal experience, just trust me that they respond well when given a concrete task, especially one that makes them feel needed and important. It's useful to remember this because it reaches into all areas of life. For example, asking your partner's advice on how to handle a thorny work problem will likely increase his participation and enhance his investment in your career. Likewise, asking for his suggestions on how to get the baby to sleep through the night, how to lose the five pounds that are ruining your life, or whether you should spend the time and money to take a painting class are all ways to engage and involve him in the way he likes best: giving advice. Men love to give advice, so give him something he does easily and well, and he may amaze you, both by becoming far more interested as well as by offering helpful and worthwhile suggestions.

Taking Turns is the second simple solution. This may seem elementary, but you have a better shot at your partner acting supportive by promoting reciprocity rather than by competing for attention. Here's a typical scenario.

You've both had a long, hard day at work. He had to fire six longtime employees, and you had your annual review, which you'd been fairly anxious about. You sit down for dinner, and both of you start talking at once, interrupting one another instead of listening to what the other is saying. Here again, fair or not, you might want to let him go first, at least this time. This doesn't mean you always have to play second fiddle, but if you can afford to wait, go ahead and wait, making sure to give him your undivided attention.

Now, here's the real challenge: How long can you wait? If your partner is really bent out of shape over having to fire his employees, especially since one was a close friend, you may want to let him process this all the way through dinner and into dessert, even though you're bursting to tell him about your review. Or you may just want to wait until you sense he's finished, clean up from dinner, and bring up your review after the ten o'clock news, once both of you have had time to relax and regroup. It's easier to wait your turn if you make sure your line items are going to end up on the agenda sooner rather than later. This is simple. Before starting dinner, tell him you're dying to know how it went at work while reminding him that some-time before bed you'd like to tell him about your review.

Ultimately, the goal is to take turns, which requires that both of you exercise patience, restraint, and respect for the importance of what each of you has to share. You can elicit this behavior by being a good example. If this doesn't work, then you'll have to be more explicit—back to asking. In this case, all you have to do is let your partner know that you want to spend some time, in this case, telling him about your review. BE SPECIFIC. If you want this to take place tonight, say tonight; don't be vague about the timing.

If you know you want at least an hour of his attention, don't tell him it will take fifteen minutes or try to talk to him between innings. Ask for what you want and then stick to your part of the deal. Don't wait until he's half-asleep to bring up the topic, and don't drown him in details for two and a half hours when you've promised to be brief. It's always wise to cover yourself by asking for a little more than what you'll need, for instance, ask for thirty minutes of his undivided attention if you're pretty sure that it won't take more than twenty.

Even if you do a good job of taking turns—being aware of timing and avoiding being competitive and overwhelming him with details—your partner still may not deliver as much support and encouragement as you would hope for. Now what?

You have two good options, and both are important resources regardless of how much or how little support you get from your mate. The first strategy is to EXPAND YOUR SUPPORT SYSTEM. Although we've covered this ground more than once, it's important to stop trying to get all or even the majority of your encouragement from your partner. Friends, coworkers, or a formal support group complement and compensate for what your partner doesn't, can't, or won't provide. While it's important to update him, why deluge your partner with the latest work-scandal drama when your coworkers can't wait to gossip about it? Why let your mate diminish your pride about your career, parenting, or other involvement when you can count on your best friend to share your enthusiasm? Why settle for "That's nice, honey" when you know you can make one phone call and get "That's incredible. Tell me everything!" If your mate isn't attentive to your interests, whether he only gives you token attention or blatantly blows you off (shame on him!), then it's up to you to share your feelings with other people who are eager and able to offer support.

Diversifying our resources makes sense, but it's something women have to make a conscious effort to do because it requires relinquishing our romantic desire to share everything with our partner and forces us to accept the limitations of our relationship. But going beyond our relationship for some aspects of what we need and want is smart and empowering. It's essential for us to know that WE HAVE CHOICES—that our mate isn't our sole source of support—and often, he's not the right or the best resource to turn to.

And, remember, the most important and reliable resource is ourselves. We can experiment with the simple solutions above, but whether they do or don't make a marked improvement in our partner's involvement and support, what truly counts is to BE PROUD OF OURSELVES. Other people—our partner, our friends, and our therapist—can help us sort through our problems and cheer us on in any number of ways. But in the final analysis, our finest, most bedrock source of support needs to come from within. If we feel insecure about our choices, we will continue to need too much external reassurance and reinforcement. If we truly feel right about our choices and proud of who we are, our mate's or friends' encouragement is just frosting on the cake.

When we're self-assured, no one can shake our fundamental sense of confidence and security. Naturally, we all have times when we feel shaky or question our choices. I'm not for total self-sufficiency; needing and being needed is a human gift with immeasurable rewards. But the more we can tap our inner strength, the less vulnerable we are if and when our partner lets us down in this area. We refuse to allow our achievements to be diminished; we don't permit our partner or anyone else to bring us down. As one of my favorite quotes by Eleanor Roosevelt goes: "No one can make you feel inferior without your consent." It's true. The simplest, most successful, and most far-reaching solution is to KEEP BUILDING OURSELVES UP so that no matter how much or little support comes from our partner, we know who we are, what we're made of, and keep cultivating self-respect.

ON THE BRIGHT SIDE

This one's a challenge. Let's see, there must be something positive about having a partner who's disinterested or unsupportive of what matters most in your life. I've got it! There are two silver linings to this cloud. First, when our partner doesn't provide the encouragement and involvement we're seeking, we're forced to look beyond our relationship, which diversifies our resources and widens our circle of support. Second, our mate's lack of support may propel us to find more of our strength and confidence within ourselves instead of depending on external approval. Trust me, this is a gift. No matter how much our partner does or doesn't overtly value our career, friendships, hobbies, and so forth, what truly matters is our own confidence in our choices. Plus, the more we turn inward, the less dependent we are on our partner to support and encourage us, which often results in his coming through, since he no longer feels pressured. How about that? See, there's always something to be thankful for.

11

If he mysteriously disappears when it's time for the kids' bath (or fails to take responsibility for other familial, social, or community involvement)

———◆———

This chapter could just as easily be entitled "If he mysteriously disappears when it's time to put our two-year-old in time-out, if he's nowhere to be found when our eleven-year-old won't study for his math test, if he wouldn't be caught dead selling raffle tickets for our annual couples' club fund-raiser, if he refuses to help address Christmas cards, if he complains about having to help move your parents into the nursing home . . ." You get the idea. (Note: Although much of this chapter is focused on parenting issues, many of the same dynamics and solutions apply to other, equally important, ways in which your mate may be slacking off in familial, social, and community commitments.)

I'll start with a parenting example. My children are now thirteen and nearly sixteen years old. I can honestly say that both before and since their father, Gary, and I divorced, he has been totally involved in every aspect of parenting, from changing diapers to driving car pools, from getting up in the middle of the night when they were babies to taking our daughter shopping for her first prom dress. I consider myself fortunate. However, so as not to magnify his contribution, Gary and I still butt heads over numerous parenting decisions, usually related to a gap in our perceptions as to what our children need. For example, at the sign of the first frost, I'm apt to frantically search the storeroom for Evan's winter boots, whereas Gary might take a cursory look or make Evan find them himself. If Evan can't find them, I'm off to the shopping mall while Gary is apt to say, "Tough. If a thirteen-year-old can't find his boots then his feet will just be wet." Or if Zoe spends all of her allowance and doesn't have pocket money to take on a synagogue retreat, I'll slip her a twenty, unable to bear the thought of my daughter going hungry even though her father is right in saying that she's old enough to budget her money. It's not that Gary is cold-hearted or that I'm totally overindulgent, although I do tend to be overprotective when it comes to my children. The real point is that Gary and I, by virtue of our different genders, interpret our parenting roles differently, which I presume is the case for most women and men.

Differences aside, with each passing year more and more men are becoming more actively involved fathers, as well as taking on greater responsibility on a variety of domestic fronts. My fantasy is that if I were writing this book ten years from now, I wouldn't even have to include this section. I expect by the time my son, Evan, becomes a father (if he chooses to do so), this material will seem old-fashioned and outdated. In the book he and his sister recently published, *Divorce Is Not the End of the World: Zoe and*

Evan's Coping Guide for Kids, when talking about custody, Evan writes: "Here's what I don't get: Lots of times, the courts just decide that kids should live with moms, which I think is incredibly stupid and sexist. It should be abolished. If both your parents are good parents, then either of them can take care of you just fine." My son's words give me hope for the upcoming generation of men, who, if they're anything like Evan, will assume full and equal responsibility for parenting.

But we've still got a long way to go, as a recent party for my friend Martha illustrates. It was Martha's birthday, and her husband, Michael, had invited a dozen or so friends for an impromptu surprise party. A bunch of us were sitting around their dining room table while one of their friends, a new mom with a six-day-old baby, paced back and forth, trying to get her daughter to settle down. Her husband, your typical proud new father, was reaching for another piece of pizza when this exhausted-looking new mom glanced at him, then looked at the other five or six women in the room, who all happened to be veteran moms, and said, "How come he's eating pizza while I'm holding the baby?" We shared knowing glances, cracked up, and replied in unison: "Get used to it."

Regardless of the strides taken in the right direction, I've come to the conclusion that on some level, all mothers are single mothers. Similarly, most women are still assuming the bulk of responsibility in handling time-consuming family plans and social and community involvement, while in many cases also handling a career. With the rare exception of men who stay home with kids while the mom works outside the home, the majority of child care still seems to fall on the shoulders of women. And it doesn't seem to matter whether we have a full-time career, divide our time between work and mothering, or are primarily at home raising our kids. No matter how great a father our mate is, most women still end up doing the majority of hands-on parenting, be it feeding babies, organizing play groups, making bag lunches, disciplining unruly adolescents, or managing the emotional outbursts of teenagers and young adults. Most men still pick and choose how they spend their time and energy, while women take on myriad demands as a matter of course. Too many men still call it "baby-sitting" when they are in charge of their own children. Too many men still think it's a "favor" to give us a half hour to take a leisurely shower before company arrives, even though we've spent three hours straightening up and making hors d'oeuvres. Too many men still assume it's up to women to settle sibling disputes, handle holiday shopping, care for aging parents, and take time off from work when our kids are sick or need to go to the doctor.

This is a big issue in that it not only affects women, who are already stressed to the max, but also denies men the rewards inherent in taking responsibility, whether it comes from forging a closer relationship with their children, experiencing the pleasure of organizing fun social plans with friends, or feeling the deep satisfaction of being there for their own parents, whose needs increasingly manifest themselves with time. Plus, in the parenting arena, it mustn't go without saying that, at present, many, many women are raising children alone, for which they deserve our highest respect and any and all the support we can offer. So it is even more unacceptable when a child is fortunate enough to have two parents but only one is taking on the lion's share of responsibility. Why, as we approach the millennium, is this still an issue? And why do we, as women, continue to accept it as the norm?

WHY ARE THEY LIKE THIS?

When it comes to parenting, one commonly accepted explanation for underinvolved fathers is the same old "gender" argument, that is, women have a natural instinct for parenting that is genetically absent in men. Parts of this make sense to me, but overall it just doesn't fly. Having carried two children in my womb, I understand why it may seem as if women have a deeper, more inherent bond with their children, having literally spent almost a year feeling them move, kick, and inhabit your very being. The constant, immediate, symbiotic presence of a baby is an incomparable experience that may have some bearing on men's having a less intimate bond with their newborns.

So far, so good. Now it's time to play devil's advocate, to punch a few pretty convincing holes in this argument: If pregnancy creates a unique bond that sets up mothers to be primary caregivers, then what about adoptive mothers, who are just as in love and involved with their children? And, even if in the first year or two moms are more involved, especially if they're nursing, why does this dynamic continue on into childhood, adolescence, and beyond? More to the point, why do men assume a lesser degree of responsibility in others areas outside of parenting, for which there is no conceivable biological or genetic explanation?

In the parenting arena, the "primal bonding" argument, while being justifiable in some respects, doesn't tell the whole story. A better explanation is that during pregnancy and/or the early stages of motherhood, women tend to take on the role of primary caregiver, which then sets up several patterns. Whereas most men go back to work shortly after the birth of their baby, most women take a maternity leave or cut back to part-time and thereby end up spending more time with the baby. As women take on primary responsibility, including nursing and/or feeding, diapering, burping, and other newborn maintenance, men either end up on the sidelines or see themselves as "fill-in" rather than essential caregivers. As mothers assume the primary role, fathers tend to back off, either because they feel expendable, incompetent, or insecure about how to care for their child. If this pattern continues, men become increasingly accustomed to seeing themselves as second-string parents, which reinforces their belief that it's okay to remove themselves from primary parenting responsibilities.

Once this pattern is established, it carries on into each stage of parenting. Our roles become calcified: Moms end up feeling overly responsible for parenting, while fathers end up not being involved enough. Add to this the fact that few men say their fathers, uncles, or other significant role models were actively involved in their upbringing, and it's easy to see why so many men still aren't nearly involved enough with their children. And often, the ones who do see parenting as their equal responsibility are either inconsistent or fall into one of two categories, both of which are unhealthy and unfair to women and men.

The first is the traditional "tough-guy Dad" versus "soft, nurturing Mom," in which women do all the caregiving while men are expected to be the disciplinarians. Sadly, some thirty years since leaving my parents' home, I now hear plenty of my contemporaries still saying the words: "Wait until your father comes home" when their children misbehave. (It was a lousy setup then, and it's still a lousy setup.) The message our kids get is: "You can walk all over your mom, but you're going to have to answer to your father." The other, equally destructive, gender role we're still playing out in 1999 is "fun Dad" versus "strict Mom." This scenario, still operating in too many contemporary families, goes something like this: Mom makes the rules, insists on teeth being brushed, rooms being cleaned, homework being finished, and chores being done, all of which is a thankless but necessary job. Meanwhile, Dad is an entertaining reprieve from Mom's nagging. Even if he acts as reinforcement, saying "Listen to your mom," he gets to take over on weekends, with outings to the mall or trips to the water slide while we are seen as "bad cop" all week long. Extending this example beyond parenting issues, the same scenario is played out when, for example, we agree to weekend plans with friends and then take the rap when our partner complains about having to see a boring play, even after giving his consent; or when it's time for the neighborhood crime watch meeting and he grumbles as dozens of people show up at our house, even though we agreed to host the meeting and all he has to do is take coats and be polite.

Whether our partner's lack of responsibility is the result of upbringing, cultural conditioning, or just plain laziness, changing this pattern takes mutual effort between ourselves and our mates, which is why we need to look at our part in contributing to this particular issue.

HOW WE MAKE IT WORSE

Again, starting with parenting, from the moment we became pregnant (or began adoption proceedings) we may have been the most driving force in setting up this pattern. Why? Because just like men, we, too, have been conditioned to think of mothers as the primary caregivers, making it entirely natural for us to have taken on the majority of parenting, while allowing—even expecting and encouraging—our mates to play a secondary role.

One typical way we do this is by *taking on so much responsibility—in parenting and in other ways—that our partner feels expendable.* Without meaning to, we may do so much that he feels as if he can't compete, and even if he tried, he couldn't do half as good a job, so why bother? When he does involve himself, we may interfere or criticize his efforts, which naturally pushes him away. For example, out of concern for our child, we sometimes forget about our partner's feelings. I can't count the times I've seen a new dad diaper or burp his baby, only to have his wife show him the "right" way, hover over him, or even take the baby out of his arms, saying something like, "That's too tight" or "If you hold her this way, it just gives her more gas." Now really. Who can blame him for giving up when every other time he tries he is made to feel inadequate?

Whenever we criticize or co-opt our partner's efforts— or he does the same to us—the natural response is to back off and stop trying. I experienced this years ago when I was married to Gary. At that time, he was a gourmet chef who'd worked in the restaurant business for years. My house specialty was tuna casserole, and even then, I sometimes burned the noodles. As a young bride, I wanted to impress him with my cooking. But . . . every time I'd make dinner, he'd stand over me in the kitchen, instructing me, correcting me, sometimes even ridiculing me until I hung up my apron and didn't pick up a colander for twelve years until I met Joey, who appreciated and liked my cooking.

We can't have it both ways. If we want our mate to be a more cooperative parent, we have to step back and let him do it his way, which I'll elaborate on in a moment. The only times we should take over instead of encouraging our partner's involvement is if our child's safety or well-being is at risk. By at risk, I'm referring to parental behavior that involves neglect or abuse, not Susie having frozen pizza instead of a balanced meal or Ricky's essay having spelling mistakes because his father helped but forgot to proofread.

But first, a quick look at another way in which we may unwittingly cause our mate to be less involved than he could be. One error we make is in being unaware or insensitive to how our relationship with our children affects their father. Early in motherhood, our bond with our baby may be so intense and exclusive that our partner simply feels left out. This feeling may intensify once our baby is born and we're absorbed in the magical intimacy of motherhood. This is an incredibly sweet time, but we run the risk of becoming so intimate with our baby that we aren't emotionally available to our mate. This isn't intentional on our part. Between being madly in love with our baby and being so exhausted that we can hardly see (don't even get me started on our culture's lack of support for new moms!), our partner simply ends up getting the leftovers and feeling like the odd man out. Often this is temporary, but in many cases, the intimate relationship between mother and child deepens as they grow older, causing fathers to withdraw further from taking an active, involved role in parenting. This can occur for a variety of reasons, including our partner being so involved in his career that he misses out on not only the spontaneous Kodak moments but also in the mundane, yet sometimes miraculous, day-to-day experiences of parenting.

But it can also occur as a result of our creating intimacy

with our kids to compensate for what's missing in our relationship with our partner, especially if the magic and romance between us has diminished or died. Immersing ourselves in motherhood—whether it's out of loneliness, frustration, boredom, or the need for meaning and purpose—alienates our mate and reinforces his lack of parenting involvement. We may even go a step further, consciously or unconsciously asserting our supremacy by thinking of ourselves as the "better" and/or more essential parent, even going so far as to communicate this to our kids. This isn't fair to them, nor is it fair to your partner. *Anytime our mate feels marginal, he's far less likely to pitch in and put effort into being a father.*

Finally, we make it harder for our partner to be a participatory father when we act like an Indispensable Woman, the term I've coined for a woman taking on more than her share because it's easier to do it herself. When raising kids we often act this way. We don't trust him to feed the baby, so we get up three times a night, even though we're not nursing and could easily be taking turns. We ask him to get our six-year-old dressed for her birthday party, then change her clothes because we want her to wear the sailor suit, instead of the overalls he's chosen. I know it's hard, but this just has to stop! Either we keep doing it all, in which case we have to stop complaining about it, or we let him do it his way even if we have to bite our tongue until it bleeds. We must alter our own behavior if we believe that it's important for our mate to be a more involved parent, and that it isn't fair for us to do it all, which it isn't, especially given that it's his child, too!

Along the same lines, if we want our partner to take on more responsibility in our extended family, then we have to take a step back and be honest about the ways in which we may be overly critical of his efforts. For example, let's say you've been in charge of buying Christmas gifts for your (and his) extended families for the past twelve years. No one appointed you and no one's ever thanked you, but somehow you ended up playing Santa Claus. Year after year you've asked your husband to go shopping with you. Year after year he refuses, and to make matters worse, complains about how much money you spend. You're fed up. This year you insist that he at least take responsibility for buying the gifts for his parents and siblings. Sounds like a deal. You've finally taken a stand, which is terrific, expect for one small problem: When he comes home and shows you what he's bought you throw a fit, which quickly escalates into an all-out fight.

Granted, you wouldn't think of buying his mother an eight-dollar picture frame at Walgreens. And you're mortified at the thought of your wealthy sister-in-law unwrapping the Whitman sampler he picked up at the checkout lane. Now what? You can return all the gifts and start over or you can bite your tongue and commend your husband for finally pitching in. How you respond in this sort of situation depends, in part, on how angry you are at your mate. Even when he does start taking steps in the right direction, months or years of stored-up resentment may get in the way of appreciating his efforts and lead you to say, "A day late and a dollar short."

WHAT HOOKS US

If it seems as if we are being unduly hard on our partners, just think about how incredibly frustrating it is to keep waiting and hoping that men will take on equal responsibility, only to be disappointed again and again. Of course it infuriates us when our partners bail out—and it should. Why? For two very good reasons: first, because we end up doing twice the work; and, second, because we interpret their lack of involvement as meaning they don't care enough about us or our relationship.

The last thing we need is more work. But what else can we do when our children, friends, or relatives need attention and our partner is either absent, irresponsible, or refuses to help out? Each time our mate abdicates responsibility, our workload increases. If, for example, there are five car pools to drive in one week and he's only willing to do one, we're left with the rest. It's not complicated—you do the math. You'd be angry if your coworkers disappeared in the midst of an important project and you ended up having to spend all weekend in order to make the deadline; similarly, it's galling to knock ourselves out when our partner could easily lessen our load.

Although, again, it's worthwhile to point out that your partner's behavior isn't necessarily a reflection of his love or commitment, it's natural to interpret it as a conspicuous lack of caring on his part. As Terese, vice president of a marketing firm and the mother of six-year-old twins, says, "Both Bill and I work full-time, and yet when we get home, I end up making dinner, getting the boys bathed, in their pajamas, and ready for bed while Bill relaxes in front of the TV. I've tried talking to Bill about how unfair it seems, and once in a while he pitches in but only when I get really pissed, which frankly takes more energy than just doing it myself. He obviously doesn't care about me or he'd help without my having to start a fight," she adds.

Maybe so, maybe not. There may be various reasons for Bill's lack of involvement. Although at first glance it's tempting to accuse him of being selfish and uncaring, there are a variety of other interpretations: He's oblivious and genuinely doesn't realize how much needs to be done. He is so overworked that he's thoroughly overwhelmed at the thought of doing one more thing. He innocently assumes that the kids fall into your job description, so it doesn't occur to him to take a more active role. (None of these excuse him, and yes, I'm bending over backward to give him the benefit of the doubt just to make a point.) Whatever the reasons for your mate's inexcusable behavior, it may have little or nothing to do with his feelings toward you. But it's still disrespectful, and it still hurts.

Finally, we find it just plain crazy—even bizarre—when our partner avoids responsibilities that we take on without blinking an eye. It's obvious to anyone that a father should change his infant's diapers, read his toddler bedtime stories, and test his fourth-grader for her spelling bee—*without being asked!* It doesn't take a genius to figure out that men should help clean up after a dinner party, or call their seventy-year-old mother once a week, or . . . or . . . or . . .

In other words, we're baffled and befuddled by what to make of our mate's behavior in this area. If women are angry it's because we feel cheated, unappreciated, and exasperated by what, to us, appears utterly indefensible. And then, to make matters worse, we end up defending ourselves, explaining why he should do what should be obvious in the first place.

No matter how many excuses he makes—or how many excuses we make to ourselves—deep down we can't find any good reason why our partner should be absolved of parenting and other important responsibilities. Women repeatedly say "She's his daughter, too, so why should I have to ask him to give her a bath?" or "They're his relatives, so why am I the one who's making Thanksgiving dinner while he reads his favorite magazine?" Unless we have an explicit agreement with our mate that it's our role to take on most or all of the parenting or other tasks, we feel understandably angry when he spends three hours at the health club when we are the ones who really need a break.

And here's the worst part: In this, as in other areas of our lives, we don't even get the benefit of his appreciation. The least he could do is acknowledge all the effort that went into making our son's birthday party or compliment us for doing a great job organizing our church's food shelf drive. So how do we get our mate to improve in this area? We can tell him, show him, explain what we want a million times in a million different ways, but the best way for our partner to learn is through experience, which he can only get if we are willing to step aside, despite our feelings and judgments regarding his behavior. It's a trade-off, and it has tangible rewards, which are only possible if we try some of the following simple solutions.

SIMPLE SOLUTIONS

Let's start with parenting. First, if you're a new mom reading this book, PREVENT THIS PATTERN FROM DEVELOPING BEFORE IT BECOMES THE STATUS QUO. Assume that you and your partner are equally responsible for caring for your child, and whatever agreements you make, be sure that they are equitable. If you're a veteran mom, it's time to examine your own choices and decide whether you're willing to make some changes.

The first is to sit down with your partner and DEFINE

YOUR PARENTING ROLES. Any division of labor is fine as long as it works for both of you. Some couples both work full-time and take turns caring for their child at night and on weekends; some agree that one parent will assume more of the daily demands, whereas the other will take over on weekends, and still other couples set their lives up so that one partner or the other (usually the male) works full-time and financially supports the family while the other (usually the female) does the majority of child care. Any arrangement is workable but only if it works for both of you.

Once again, it's time to NEGOTIATE. If you feel that you're doing too much and he isn't doing enough, then you'll need to bring this up to your partner. At the risk of repeating myself, make every effort to approach him respectfully rather than reading him the riot act. No matter how angry you feel, take a time-out before throwing a full-scale temper tantrum, even if he walks in from work, you ask him to watch the baby while you change clothes, and he says: "I've been working all day, what have you been doing?"

Excuse me? I say let's eliminate the term "working mother" from the English language. *Every mother is a working mother.* Period. So, as you enter into negotiations, don't buy into the argument that he's working and you're not. And keep in mind: The best working arrangements are those in which each individual does what he or she enjoys the most and does the best. For example, if you're nursing (obviously he can't do that!), then maybe he should take over the nightly bath. Or if he enjoys and is available to coach Little League, let him do that, while in exchange, you might agree to be in charge of supervising homework. Taking turns is, of course, one of the best ways to even things out. For example, my ex-husband, Gary, and I take turns taking our son, Evan, to his monthly orthodontist appointments, which is fair, since to do so we each have to take time out of our busy schedules. But in other ways, we've had to devise a creative job-sharing arrangement that accommodates Gary's schedule. When he's out of town, I've agreed to be responsible for the kids, which he then compensates for by giving me the weekend off or taking a few extra days later on down the road. Even when he is in town, I'm the first call for help in case one of our kids comes home sick from school or needs to be driven somewhere, since I work at home and have a more flexible schedule. I realize that ours is an unusually good working arrangment, but trust me, we've worked at it, sometimes bickering over the fine points, arguing over who's doing more, struggling to find a compromise, but always trying to take both our own needs and our children's into account.

Negotiation is necessary and compromise is our only hope of increasing our partner's parenting involvement. But even as you work at a more equitable arrangement, don't expect it to be fifty-fifty, or even close. Still, depending on your current division of labor, your particular partner, and the degree to which you have or haven't expected him to participate in the past, his commitment to any increased involvement is worth your effort. State clearly that you expect more active parenting on his part, but DON'T EXPECT MIRACLES and don't expect him to suddenly turn into Mr. Mom. Go for small, gradual improvements, and as always, be specific in your requests, such as, "Please remove those earplugs and go handle Tommy's tantrum" or "I'd like you to pick Lindsay up from play practice Wednesday at five."

If it irritates you to have to ask or remind him, remember your objective: to encourage your mate to be a more participatory father, which requires repressing the temptation to be snotty or blaming, even though you and I both know he shouldn't have to be asked or reminded to take responsibility for his own children, your mutual friends, or either of your extended families.

Another easy way to increase his participation is to AC-TIVELY INVOLVE HIM MORE in parenting and other activities. Sometimes, especially if we've spent years acting and feeling like "single mothers" even when we're married or living with our children's father, we just give up and go about parenting as if our mate doesn't exist. We stop inviting him to join us at our children's school conferences or extracurricular activities. We don't tell him about the adorable or awful things they do. We handle disciplinary problems without asking his opinion. We make plans with our children without including him or make decisions without seeking his input. In short, we leave him out of the loop, either because we're tired of having to wait for him to take the initiative, because we don't trust his parenting skills, or because we're so furious and frustrated we've finally given up, figuring that if he isn't going to be a good father, it's his loss.

"I want Scott to take more responsibility for our three-year-old son, Charlie, but every time I leave him in charge it's a disaster," explains Heather. "I end up coming home to an exhausted child who should have been put to bed two hours ago and a husband barking at me when I ask why he's in his darkroom developing pictures while Charlie's half asleep in front of a video," Heather says. "I've told Scott when and how to put Charlie to bed. I've explained how there's this small window of opportunity, fifteen minutes after Charlie's bath, when he's relaxed and is ready to hear a bedtime story and fall asleep, and if he doesn't do it then, we can count on an hour-long ordeal with a crabby, overtired child. I may as well be talking to the wall. Either Scott just doesn't get it or he doesn't care, but I can't deal with the consequences, so I've just stopped going out until after I've gotten Charlie into bed. Otherwise this is what I come home to."

A familiar refrain—one I've heard from hundreds of women. I'd love to promise you that if we let go of control, our mate will take charge and do an effective job of parenting, but the furthest I can go is to say that THE MORE WE GET OUT OF OUR PARTNER'S WAY, THE MORE HE'LL LEARN ABOUT WHAT DOES AND DOESN'T WORK. That's the only way to learn. So to whatever degree you can, try to set aside your anger and include him however and whenever you can. Tell him exactly when your ob-gyn appointment is and let him know how excited you are for him to hear the baby's heartbeat. Keep him apprised of every aspect of your children's activities, especially what's going on at school, and whenever possible, put him in charge. For instance, have him help your fifth-grader make the papier-mâché volcano, and make him (let him) be the one who takes your kids shopping for school supplies or helps them pack for camp.

Similarly, you might temporarily or even permanently shift some of your other social and familial responsibilities over to your mate. Another strategic tip: *Men like to be in charge.* The more positive experiences your mate has as a proud and competent father, devoted son, or committed friend, the more responsibility he'll take on without your having to beg, complain, or explain.

Since lack of confidence may be part of why he doesn't

participate, it's helpful to SHOW YOUR PARTNER HOW TO BE MORE EFFECTIVE. But exercise caution! Taking on the role of "teacher" is a risky business that can make a positive difference if he's open and you're extremely careful or can turn into an absolute nightmare if you appear in the least bit patronizing or bossy. It takes real skill to demonstrate, show, or teach him how to correctly swaddle an infant, get a school-aged kid to bed without a fight, or handle a teenager's sullenness or rebelliousness without increasing his feelings of insecurity. You say, "Honey, Jimmy needs two extra pairs of socks and his warm gloves before you take him sledding," and, sure enough, your partner hears, "Stupid idiot. It's fifteen below zero and you're taking him out like that?" The solution? Try, "Honey, thanks so much for taking Jimmy sledding. Be sure he's dressed warm enough," and then leave it at that. Be casual. Support his effort. And then hope he has the common sense to dress his son appropriately. It's more important that your partner take on more responsibility and form a closer bond with your child than whether or not he does everything the way we do, and naturally, the way we think he should.

And what if you try all of the above and your mate still mysteriously disappears when it's time for the kids' bath? Here's one extreme but highly effective strategy: Walk out the door and leave him in charge so that he doesn't have a choice.

This is a last resort, but it often has amazingly good results, as the following anecdote shows. After asking and asking her husband, Carl, to give her some much-needed relief from taking care of their nine-month-old daughter, Kara finally hit the wall. One night she simply turned to Carl, handed him the baby, and announced that she was meeting friends for dinner and would be back by ten. (She did slip him the number where she could be reached.) "Walking out that door was one of the hardest things I've ever done," recalls Kara, whose friends made her sit on her hands all through dinner so that she wouldn't call home. "I suffered through that dinner, but you know what?" says Kara. "I got home that night and the baby was in bed, Carl was totally blasé and bragging about how he got her down right after her last bottle, so how come I have so much trouble getting her to sleep? Right then and there I put him in charge of bedtime."

Dramatic moves sometimes pay off. Unfortunately, there are men who will never be as involved as we'd like, whether we walk on eggshells or issue ultimatums. If this describes your mate, here's something important to remember: We have only so much say over what our partner does and doesn't do. We have to continue to feel good about being the best mother we're capable of being, and accept that whatever relationship our mate does or doesn't develop with our children will have far-reaching consequences that are out of our control. In the end, he'll have to answer to himself and his children for the father he turns out to be. Meanwhile, we can get support from other moms, we can hire baby-sitters, we can say "no," or "not now," or "you'll have to wait," when we are running on empty, instead of being Super Mom and Martyr to make up for our partner's lack of participation. The net result, regardless of whether or not our mate takes his responsibilities seriously, is that our kids will remember who stayed up with them at night, who drove across town to get the last Batman costume in stock, and who was really there when it counted. They may adore their dad even if he didn't make a fraction of the effort you did, but take comfort in knowing that your children, especially as they get older, are well aware of all the ways in which you are there. As are your friends, relatives, and all the other people who appreciate the ways you give, even if you wish your partner would give a little—or a lot—more.

ON THE BRIGHT SIDE

Although we complain about our partner's lack of active participation, you have to agree there are some real advantages to being a "single" mother, even when our children's father is watching television in the next room. Our time with our children is precious (and often exhausting), and there is a certain rhythm to our mothering that gets interrupted by our partner's involvement. I can't count the number of women who, when their partner has left town on business or pleasure, say what a welcome break it is to be alone with their children. (Never mind getting the whole bed to yourself!) As Emily, whose kids are five and seven, says, "When it's just me and the kids, everything goes so smoothly. They know what to expect, and we have our own way of doing things, whether it's homework or our bedtime ritual. Then, when Ted comes home, everything gets screwed up. I'm not saying that my way is better than his way, just that his presence changes the natural flow between me and the kids."

This sentiment, whether related to familial, social, or community involvement, is shared by many women. Ideally, we'd find the right balance between our partner's participation and how much time we want to devote to these endeavors. Meanwhile we can savor the times when we're in charge, when we make the rules, and mostly, when we enjoy our mastery as mothers and our satisfaction at giving what we truly want to give.

12

If he has a three-minute attention span when talking about feelings

Y ou've been mulling it over for the past three days. You've discussed it with your best friend, your therapist, and anyone else who'll listen. You've carefully thought through your timing and your approach. You've practiced in front of the mirror, and you've prepared yourself for the possibility of this getting nasty. You take a deep breath, steel yourself, and say, "Honey, there's something we need to talk about."

Congratulations! You've just landed the leading role in your partner's worst nightmare: The "we have to talk about our relationship" scene.

It doesn't seem to matter whether they're seventeen or thirty-seven, boys and men seem to have a fundamental aversion to talking about feelings, especially any that may provoke a serious conversation about the status of your relationship. Are they intimacy impaired? Or, as my fifteen-year-old daughter, Zoe, recently asked, "Are they just idiots, Mom?" Zoe had just slammed down the phone after a conversation with her most recent boyfriend. The boy, who just last night had confessed his undying love, was now feeling "a little pressured and not really ready for a relationship." The prom date, for which Zoe had just bought her first long black dress, was off. So much for undying love.

But here's the interesting part. Zoe wasn't upset over this boy's change of heart, nor was she angry about being "dumped" or left dateless for the prom. What pissed her off was this boy's refusal to talk about the situation. I could hear her on the phone, having literally the same conversation I, you, and most women have had more times than we care to remember. In brief, Zoe was trying to get the boy to tell her his real feelings, (first mistake). He, of course, was doing everything he could to get off the phone, but like all of us, she persisted. "Whatever you feel is okay," she assured him in her best social worker voice (second mistake), which appeared to quickly end the conversation. Meanwhile, I'm ready to kill this boy, and she's being thoughtful and considerate about his feelings just to keep him on the line.

"Are they *all* like this?" asked Zoe as she and her best friends sprawled on my bed, expectantly awaiting my reply. What could I say? Do I tell my daughter that most, if not all, men are somewhat screwed up when it comes to handling emotional intimacy? It breaks my heart to burst her bubble or encourage cynicism at such a young, tender age. On the other hand, isn't it part of my job as her mother to prepare her for real life, so that she'll have the advantage of appropriate expectations as she enters into more serious relationships?

The whole scene saddens me. I'd give anything to honestly assure my daughter that it's possible to have an emotionally healthy relationship with a man. But she also deserves the benefit of my experience. And my experience has shown me that men, in general, rail against talking about feelings and getting into "heavy" issues that we bring up.

They'd get a few brownie points if they were at least able to be honest about their reluctance or refusal to process feelings. "I can't or I don't want to talk about this" isn't the ideal, but it's a start. More typically, they react in one of the following ways:

- ACTING LIKE THEY'RE NOT THERE. When all else fails, men check out. They get that glazed look in their eyes, suddenly remember they have an urgent phone call to make, or in some other way manage to extricate themselves from the situation.
- ACTING LIKE A JERK. Mocking you, accusing you of making a big deal out of nothing, or acting like you're overly needy when you're not.
- ACTING SUPERIOR. Telling you to "lighten up" or brandishing the *S* word, saying, "You're too sensitive," or better yet, the *I* word, accusing you of being "too intense," yet another one of those hip new male buzz words used to disarm, devalue, and diminish the weight of your feelings.
- ACTING PATRONIZING. Telling us "not to take it personally," which for the life of me I've never been able to figure out. It's a good try, but frankly this is one of men's stupidest moves. First they're emotionally distant or verbally abusive to you; then, they tell you that it isn't personal.

- ACTING CONDESCENDING. It's not meant as a put-down, but most men respond to emotional intensity by giving advice or finding some way to "fix" our problem. We just want them to listen, and they want to repair us so we'll shut up and they'll be off the hook.

- PLEADING GUILTY. This one's a clever disguise. You muster up the courage to tell him you're upset about something he's done. He hangs his head in shame and mutters, "You're right. I'm a jerk." Great. That does you a lot of good. Especially since he seems to think this is the end rather than the beginning of a conversation.

- ACTING INTIMIDATING. Everything's going along smoothly, and then suddenly we bring up an issue that's so glaring we can't believe he isn't troubled as well. What are the chances he might say, "Thank you for bringing this up. It's so helpful for us to talk about this"? Not very high. He probably would say, "You know, if we're going to spend all our time analyzing our problems, I'm not so sure I . . ." In other words, this isn't any fun.

Whatever makes men think that being in a committed love relationship is like an endless day at the beach? Once again, I'm tempted to say, "Grow up!" Deep intimate relationships are a dynamic mix of smooth sailing and troubled waters, times when we're in perfect sync and other times when difficult issues arise. Remember "for better and for worse"? The true test of a relationship's quality and endurance is not our ability to get along when we're on vacation or having great sex, but whether we can push through and remain close during hard times, and whether we end up strengthened for having shared the experience.

We've come to the most common intersection where men and women collide: The majority of women want and need to talk about their feelings. We feel closer, safer, and more connected when we're able to be self-revealing. And we want the same in return. But men just don't work this way, which creates a real dilemma. Usually this dilemma plays out as a power struggle.

Fact: In any encounter, the person who is silent has more power than the one who's spilling his or her guts. Guess which one we are? When we put ourselves on the line, we in effect relinquish some of our power, especially if we're walking on a tightrope and he's firmly on the ground.

It's another trade-off; we release our true emotions, but he ends up having the power to hurt us, which he may do by being disinterested, disdainful, or throwing our emotions back in our face. In effect, he'll do whatever necessary to shut us up so as to avoid any potential conflict or confrontation.

I'm somewhere between awed and appalled at how men are seemingly able to ignore their feelings, even when in the midst of an intensely emotional experience. Maybe they're robots or cyborgs. Whatever they are, they're unbelievably good at shelving or denying or letting go of their feelings, which is just great for them but has the power to frustrate and intimidate us.

Last summer I spent three days in a car, driving from Louis's cabin in Vermont to our separate homes in Minneapolis. The first thing I learned was that there's no good way to get from Vermont to Minneapolis. The choices are hundreds of thousands of endless miles through upper

Canada, devoid of scenery, except for an occasional lone barn; through Chicago, which means days on an interstate; or taking the Michigan ferry, which is a lovely three-hour crossing, except it only embarks at 7 A.M. and 11 P.M., which didn't fit into our schedule.

In fact, it was our schedule that provoked the fight. I'd been patiently waiting all day for Louis to be ready to get on the road. As usual, he was marching to his own drum at his usual painfully slow pace as dusk fell and it became later and later. I started out nicely asking him for an estimate of when we'd be leaving? (I'm an information junkie: Whatever it is, just tell me and I'll deal with it!) By midafternoon I was getting crabby; I mentioned that we should hurry up so that we wouldn't end up in some cheap motel in the middle of nowhere in the middle of the night. By 7 P.M. I was ballistic, so when we finally pulled out of the driveway we started our long-awaited car trip home on the worst possible note. I was furious. Didn't I at least deserve a little consideration, like being told that it's taking longer? Or perhaps he could have moved a little faster and not assumed that he was calling all the shots, since they affected me too. He was at least as angry. How could I have ruined his final hours in his New England sanctuary? We quickly escalated to character assassination: He was rude. I was rigid. He'd been indulging me for two weeks; I'd given up visiting day at my son's camp to go with him to Vermont.

After we'd exchanged a number of nasty things not worth repeating, we each settled into our separate corners. He turned on the radio; I picked up my magazine, pretending to read while I struggled to sort through my feelings. For the next thirty miles or so, he made small talk, as if everything was peachy keen. Finally, I couldn't stand it. I offered the peace pipe, saying that I thought we were both partly right and partly wrong. I apologized for having pressured him, adding that I really did feel disregarded. "So are we okay?" I asked. His response was, "I think we've beaten it into the ground. Can we just have a nice ride the rest of the way home?" The next two hundred miles were spent in silence. I have never felt more alone in my life. I was scared to say anything, knowing that what I would say might be fodder for another fight. So I just shut up, feeling totally alienated, as if I didn't even know this person with whom I'd spent the last two years.

I have no idea how men do it. In my silence, I wondered to myself, Does he really think things are okay or is he just able to put it aside? I couldn't. As we pulled up to the anticipated cheap motel somewhere truly in the middle of nowhere, I offered to get us a room. I went inside the dimly lit office, registered, and paid. Louis and I walked up the stairway to the second floor; he turned to me bleary-eyed and asked, "Which room?" "This one's yours and that one's mine," I announced, handing him the key and saying good night.

I could hear him down the hall yelling, "I don't get you. I don't know what the hell is going on with you!" Before falling asleep I wrote him a six-page letter, which I left under his door. As I recall, the gist of the letter was, "Just in case you're really as clueless as you seem, maybe you're so tough or scared or stoic that you can spend seven hours in a car in the middle of a fight pretending it never happened, but I can't! And I don't want to."

It's tragic that we have to make such dramatic gestures to get our point across and to get a rise out of our partners. We'll go to great lengths to force the issue, whereas most men would rather bury, hide, ignore, and avoid talking about their feelings, and those who have learned to express their feelings are still a bit out of their league when it comes to dealing with women. When it comes to communicating feelings, women definitely have the edge. Here's where we shine; we're highly skilled and extremely fluent at expressing our emotions, which is one of the reasons women promote "feelings conversations" and men avoid them at all cost. It's not that it's fun, exactly. (My last boyfriend used to yell at me, "Maybe you think it's fun to talk about all this stuff, but I don't!") *Fun* is the wrong word. Perhaps it is necessary, stimulating, challenging, and often extremely worthwhile, but not necessarily fun. Having a deep conversation, however, does appeal to our sense of drama and our desire to be connected to our mate. Women will stay in an emotional interaction with her partner long after it's productive or positive, just to feel that he's engaged. In other words, we keep him talking, even if it's going badly, because refusing to let him check out reassures us that he's emotionally involved. Plus, let's not forget that we're trying to clear the air, get at the root of the problem, and get along better, which is why we started the conversation in the first place.

Which is exactly why most men turn us off. Whether they're sweet, sensitive guys, tough, macho types, or "never show them you're scared" kind of guys, talking about relationship issues confuses and frightens them. I feel a particular sympathy for men who came of age during the late sixties and learned how to express their feelings, but who now find themselves sitting home on Saturday night, having learned that nice guys finish last. One of the casualties of the women's movement is that a large segment of the male population ended up extremely confused about how to be a man. If you're sensitive, you're a nebbish, a nerd. If you've got an edge, you're sexy, but a potential bully or batterer. Mr. Nice Guy is a boring, predictable pushover, and Mr. Attitude isn't getting any, just because we're not about to make it easy for him. Each model has its limitations. Or, to put it more cleverly using two of my favorite quotes: "Women like silent men. They think they're listening" (Marcel Achard) and "Beware of men who cry. Men who cry are sensitive and in touch with feelings, but the only feelings they tend to be sensitive to and in touch with are their own" (Nora Ephron).

I don't buy it. Once again, men get my vote of confidence. I believe in their genuine desire to feel emotionally close and connected, even though every move they make seems choreographed to communicate the opposite. So if underneath they yearn for intimacy, why do they continue to push it away?

WHY ARE THEY LIKE THIS?

Because they're scared. Let's go back to the earlier list of ways men avoid emotional intimacy. Why is it that the second we open our mouth and look even a little bit earnest he looks away, starts running the dishwasher, has to go to the bathroom, has to run to the grocery store . . . anything, anything, to avoid the confrontation.

This is one of the problems. Any indication on our part that we want to discuss feelings is immediately assumed to be focused on problems. To him, *every conversation is a confrontation,* every "we need to talk" a potentially dangerous situation. And he's somewhat justified in his interpretation, since we often forget to include our positive feelings in conversations, instead focusing on the negative.

Again cultural conditioning must be factored in. Growing up, little boys experience little if any encouragement to express their feelings. These lessons are learned at a young age, as exemplified by an interaction my son, Evan, and I had last year. He was in big trouble. He'd changed plans three times without telling me, he'd broken plans with his grandmother, and now he wanted to be rescued when I was right in the middle of moving. I was livid, and I told him so. I explained that he had really screwed up this time and that he had to be more responsible. I asked him what he thought the consequences should be. I informed him he would start losing privileges unless he straightened up fast. In the middle of my outburst, he broke in screaming, "Fine! I screwed up! Just how long do we have to talk about it?" My heart broke as the truth sunk in. My son was becoming a man—acting out that age-old male-female scenario in which we try to engage them in emotional intercourse, and they cut us off as fast as they can.

What are men so scared of? They're scared of facing problems in their relationship. They don't want to be put on the spot, they don't want to confess, and they don't want to be backed into a corner (all animals in nature fight or flee when cornered). They don't want to hear about the ways they've hurt you. And they don't want to look at themselves.

Your mate may also resist talking about a problem because *he doesn't see it as a problem.* I know this sounds crazy, but I bet you can back me up on this one. It never ceases to amaze me in a counseling session when one partner, usually the woman, goes on and on, giving a blow by blow account of what she sees as a serious relationship issue, while her partner scratches his head and wonders why they're even talking about it. Either they're really that impervious or they actually don't emotionally react to situations in the same way or with the same intensity women do.

For whatever reason, this one's a tough nut to crack, but I'm determined to have a go at it. Again, exploring our own part in this dynamic is quite revealing.

HOW WE MAKE IT WORSE

We tell him too much! We want to tell our partner everything, but this formula doesn't work, so it's time to stop. Beside, all he wants are the Cliffs Notes, thank you very much.

I am, however, urging you to be good to yourself, which means choosing carefully when and how much of your feelings to reveal so as to get the most amount of support and risk the least possibility of being hurt.

Most of us err on the side of revealing too much, either because we can't separate the wheat from the chaff or because once we have his attention, we're not about to give up the mike. But this is a case in which "less is more." They're much more attentive when they have to work at getting us to open up (back to that conquest thing). They're far more fascinated when given little snippets of information, just enough to tantalize but not enough to exceed their tolerance level.

And *silence is the most powerful tool of all.* Use it sparingly—it totally freaks them out. Unfortunately, we're rarely silent unless we're really angry or traumatized. But notice what happens in these situations. You're driving in the car and you and your partner have just had a petty argument. You stop talking. A minute goes by. Another few. You pass an Amoco on your left and a shopping center on your right. You still haven't said a word. He clears his throat. He fidgets. He channel surfs the radio, turns it off, turns to you, and asks: "Honey, is something wrong?" Yes! You win the big brass ring.

Choosing when to open up, when to pull back, when to speak, and when to be quiet are invaluable tools that women need to learn how to use. Restraint is another. Our sense of drama and urgency may put off our partner. We want what we want and we want it now! Urgency is partly what our partner is referring to when he uses the *I* word. When we're insecure about the status of our relationship or feeling anxious about where we are at, we're more likely to be at our most intense.

Now don't misunderstand me. I'm in no way telling you to stop being strong and assertive about going after what you want. I'm not recommending that any of us regress and act (and it is an act) passive, weak, or submissive, like a character in *Jane Eyre* or a Rules Girl, trading being honest for what they call "mystery."

Personally, there's enough mystery between men and women without manufacturing gimmicks and games to keep men off balance or on their toes. Real mystery is when you look at someone you've lived with for fifteen, twenty, even fifty years, and he or she says or does something amusing or endearing that takes you utterly by surprise, and you say to yourself, After all these years, I'm still fascinated by this person.

That's mystery. There is something to be said for keeping a part of ourselves private—sacred personal territory that exclusively belongs to us. When something is sacred we treat it with great care. We don't squander it or spend it unwisely because we appreciate that it's a rarity. We neither exaggerate its value nor care whether others share our enthusiasm. We know its value—our value—and treat it accordingly.

That's how we should treat our feelings. We should share as much as feels safe and comfortable and keep the rest safely locked away, or carefully express them to someone worthy of our confidence. We should moderate our urgency and intensity, trusting in the natural timing and unfolding of events. Few conversations can't wait, and sometimes there's a better time or a better way to approach our mate.

WHAT HOOKS US

It's hard to pull back because it goes against our nature. We long to be known, to feel so confident in our relationship that we can reveal every nook and cranny of our naked self and still feel loved. I once saw the word *intimacy* spelled out in a book as *Into Me You See.* That's what we want. To whatever degree we feel we can be self-revealing (without being criticized), we feel happy and satisfied in our relationship. When we have to censor ourselves, we feel as if there must be some part of us that is too messy, ugly, or difficult for our partner to want to see. We feel as if we have to hide. We feel rejected and resentful that our partner's "I love you's" don't mean "I love everything about you," making his love seem conditional, which increases our insecurity.

In fact, he's reading us wrong. We don't actually expect our mate to love everything about us. God knows, we don't love or even like everything about ourselves, nor do we love or like everything about our mate. All we want is to feel enough trust to be who we really are—without any disguise—even if that means exposing the less attractive aspects of ourselves. We can take it. We're tough. What we can't take is the isolation and estrangement that comes from having to keep our emotions in check in order to keep our partner from blowing us off or bailing out of this very important aspect of being in a committed love relationship.

So where does this leave us? How do we approach our partner in a way that increases his willingness to talk about feelings but still keeps us safe?

SIMPLE SOLUTIONS

It's all about Respecting Ourselves. I can advise you to tell your partner half of what you normally tell him, I can suggest that you develop better boundaries, create less drama, use good timing, but in the end, it all comes down to Honoring Ourselves enough to know when it's right to share our feelings and when we are better off keeping them to ourselves.

I've been practicing talking less, especially with a certain man who seems to have an extremely limited attention span for listening to what I consider to be the marvelously compelling and entertaining details of my life. One night when he actually fell dead asleep in the middle of our (my) conversation, I finally "got it." I thought, Well this is really stupid. I'm revealing my innermost soul and sharing my brilliant epiphanies while he's snoring, totally unaware that he's with me, much less caring about what I have to say.

Now I Keep It Simple and Keep It Short. In this man's

case, I've decided that the extreme gap in our emotional conversation libido is too big to bridge, and therefore have broken up with him. Which isn't what I'm encouraging you to do.

I am, however, encouraging you to watch your tendency to go on and on and on. Women typically describe their emotional terrain in such vivid and complex terms that we end up overwhelming our partner. We don't know when to stop. We keep explaining, defending, and coming up with examples to support our position. *We don't have to support our position!* These are our feelings, not a master's thesis or campaign platform. This may not be your natural instinct, but here's a hot tip: All you have to do is say how you feel. That's it. I'm angry. I'm sad. I'm scared. If you need to elaborate, keep it to one sentence, such as "I'm angry that you criticized me in front of my parents." "I'm sad that we haven't spent any romantic time together lately." "I'm scared that we're growing apart."

When I work with aspiring authors, their first assignment is to sum up their entire book in one sentence, which is harder than it sounds. The same can work in our emotional dealings with men. Just say it, keep it brief, and then let the ball be in his court. If he picks it up, great, you can start playing. If he throws it back at you, you can either push the conversation along or decide he's unreceptive, in which case you have other choices.

One good choice is to SHARE SOME OF YOUR FEELINGS WITH SOMEONE OTHER THAN YOUR MATE. I know I'm constantly harping on the richness of female friendships, but it's one of the most reliable and rewarding sources of emotional intimacy. I've been through a few husbands and enough boyfriends and lovers to fill a memoir, but when I really need to talk, it's my women friends who are a sure bet. I can't image how I'd survive without my sister, Faith; my friends Jill, Martha, Rachel, Rita, Nancy, Bonnie; and some close male friends as well. There's just no substitute for friendship. In fact, whenever Zoe and her teenaged girlfriends sleep over, before saying good night, I always make them repeat the mantra: "Boys come and go. Girlfriends are forever."

There's also our mother, therapist, trusted coworkers, and plenty of other people who care about us, are here for us, and are eager to share our feelings and be a source of emotional support. My friend Martha has a saying I love that's perfectly apt: "Don't go to the hardware store for raisins." In other words, go where you know you have a good chance of getting what you're looking for. If you want someone to analyze your feelings, go to a therapist. If you want reassurance, try a friend. If you want emotional intimacy, and your partner doesn't have it to give, stop standing at an empty counter. Go to where the well is full—including and especially—within yourself.

Which brings us full circle. We can be our own best counselor and confidante, reducing how much or how often we turn to our partner to talk about our feelings. We can muse about them, write about them in our journal, and reflect on them to our heart's content, which often results in the only real sense of security and reassurance we're seeking. If we know what we feel, and we accept who we are, we have nothing to fear if our partner can't or won't share at this level. It doesn't mean he doesn't love you. It just means he'd rather not talk about feelings. Sometimes a cigar is just a cigar.

ON THE BRIGHT SIDE

There's a lot to be gained by seeking our own counsel. It's empowering to keep some of our feelings to ourselves and equally empowering to know when, how, and with whom to confide. I used to tell whatever man was my current lover every single detail of every single emotion I was feeling every single moment. Not only did he (same reaction across the board, more or less) eventually get that trapped animal look on his face, I'd end up feeling emotionally wasted and overly exposed. Now I'm learning to keep a certain portion of my innermost feelings private. It feels great! Why? Because I am no longer squandering my emotions by sharing them with someone who neither understands nor values the information. More importantly, I feel closer to myself and more confident in general. Protecting our emotions is no different from protecting our bodies. We wouldn't sleep with anyone without practicing safe sex, yet we may prematurely or indiscriminately share our feelings, which is also dangerous. We may not get a disease, but we run the risk of feeling embarrassed and ashamed. One of my daily affirmations right now is: "My feelings are precious. I will share them only with those who can treat them as such." Try it. It's working for me.

13

If he breaks promises faster than he makes them

———

Words are easy. After enough badgering, even the most stubborn male will give in and say what he wants us to hear. It's a survival instinct—anything to get us off his back. But promises made under duress rarely hold up. The most trustworthy promises are those made of our own volition: We're adamant about losing fifteen pounds, so we stay on our diet because we have a serious stake in the outcome. Or we promise to set aside at least one night a week as a "date night" with our partner because it's been months since we've made time for romance in our relationship. We're apt to keep our commitment because of how much we expect to gain. In contrast, when anyone, including our partner, makes promises because he's feeling pressured, backed against the wall, or as a response to an ultimatum, the chance of his keeping his word is slim to nil. Usually, promises get broken in one of three ways.

First, he promises but doesn't come through. Either he "conveniently forgets" having had the conversation or simply lets things slide until and unless we confront him on his commitment. Second, he follows through for a day, a week, but then regresses to his prior behavior. Lastly, he actually makes an effort to make good on his promise, but not without our constantly reminding and rewarding him each and every time.

Dealing with broken promises is one of the toughest relationship issues women face. It's right up there on our top-ten list of things he does that make us disappointed and disillusioned. This behavior is upsetting on a number of levels. Think about what's really going on here. We want something from our partner, which usually is appropriate to ask for. We may want him to pay more attention to us, be more involved with our kids, do more around the house, or any of the changes we've talked about throughout this book. So we want the "right" things, and then we have to make the effort to ask him to do what he "should" do without our having to ask. We present our argument, and finally he agrees, usually with a certain amount of whining and resentment. But he agrees. He gives us his word. We allow ourselves to get a little excited about his promise, and then, nine times out of ten, he breaks his promises, and we end up angrier than if we hadn't even bothered to ask.

Each time our partner makes a commitment and then abdicates responsibility, we experience a mixture of crummy feelings: We feel as if we don't count. We feel as if our partner doesn't take us or our relationship seriously. And we feel somewhat hopeless about the possibility of change.

We may feel even worse if our mate does what he says

he'll do for a while and then relapses, because we've allowed ourselves to get excited, and then, once again, we feel let down. Each time we get our hopes squashed, we lower our expectations and feel less confident of our relationship. And if our partner does what he promises, but only with our constantly reminding and rewarding him, we have mixed feelings as well. We're getting what we want, but as usual, we have to be hypervigilant, assuming the role of "mother," "manager," or "supervisor," when the whole point is for him to take more responsibility.

Here's another variation on the same theme: He makes a promise, breaks it, apologizes, and then does the same thing over again.

After a while this dynamic develops a pattern similar to that of an abusive relationship. Let me illustrate. Anna is in love with Mark. He's smart, gorgeous, tender, and sexy, except when he's drunk, which has been an ongoing problem in their relationship. It's taken Anna nearly a year and a half of dating to realize the extent of Mark's drinking problem, during which time she's tried various strategies in dealing with his alcohol use because she doesn't want to lose him. In the time they've been together, much of it wonderful, she's noticed that on several occasions Mark has been belligerent and combative, and each of these times he'd been drinking. So first, she asks him to let her know whether or not he's had too much to drink so that she can decide whether or not to be with him that night. This doesn't work, since once Mark starts on the scotch he isn't self-aware enough to give Anna a reliable status report on his condition. Next, Anna tries to figure out how much scotch it takes for Mark to be drunk. After all, they've often had dinner out, with each of them having a glass of wine or one mixed drink without any problem.

Anna wants to know whether it takes one drink, two drinks, or three drinks for Mark to cross the line from having a nice "buzz" to being obnoxious and ruining their evening. But Mark can't quantify his drinking; depending on how he's feeling, one drink can put him in an ugly, argumentative mood, while other times he can drink a lot and still be fairly cogent, pleasant, and good company. Finally, Anna tries her last resort. Without accusing him of being an alcoholic, she simply tells him that she doesn't want to be with him when he's drinking. She points out that since they don't live together and can choose when they're together, she would simply prefer to be with him when he's sober because she feels safer and has a much better time. Mark reluctantly agrees to her terms, making it clear that he resents the limitations she's placed on him. But he promises.

Three days later, Anna comes home from work and finds Mark waiting in her kitchen with flowers, fresh shrimp, and a half-empty bottle of scotch on the counter. A fight ensues, and she asks him to leave. The next morning, as usual, he leaves a heartfelt apology on her answering machine. "I'm so sorry. I really blew it. I don't deserve you and you don't deserve to have to put up with my drinking problem. I promise it won't happen again."

After half a dozen replays of the very same scenario, Anna finally comes to her senses. "I'm sorry" isn't enough anymore. As she tells a friend, "I'm sick of the 'I'm sorries.' I feel like telling Mark, yeah, you're sorry. And the next 'I'm sorry' will be 'I'm sorry I humiliated you at the party last night' or 'I'm sorry I hit you' or 'I'm sorry you're in the hospital with a broken leg from the car crash when I'd had too much to drink to be behind the wheel.'"

Personally, I have a lot of respect for the power of making amends. The words "I'm sorry," when spoken genuinely and with a real intention to make lasting changes, can dramatically improve our relationships. But "I'm sorry" can also be an easy way out.

Here's how to tell the difference between productive apologies and ones that are merely a way of temporarily smoothing things over. *If your mate makes a promise, breaks it, apologizes, and then makes a tangible effort to get with the program, then accept his apology and watch his behavior. If he's sincere, you will begin to see some of the changes you've asked for. If, however, your mate continually breaks promises, offers a token apology, and then repeats the same behavior, don't be taken in by his saying "I'm sorry." Even if he means it, it doesn't mean that anything will improve.* In fact, accepting his apology may give him the wrong message: Apologies can wipe out past indiscretions and have no bearing on future actions.

I've come to the conclusion that there's nothing more important than a man's (or woman's) word. What else do we have to go on? If we can't count on our partner to keep his promises, our trust erodes and we become increasingly estranged. Why is it so hard to expect men to say what they mean and mean what they say?

WHY ARE THEY LIKE THIS?

I must admit I'm a little stumped here, maybe because I'm the sort of person who takes promises seriously and rarely breaks them, to myself or to other people. I'm a bit perplexed as to why this seems to be so difficult for men, but I have a few clues.

For starters, this goes back to men's stubborn resistance

to answer to women. This is somewhat convoluted, but often, even if they want to do what we've asked, *men will resist agreeing to our terms as a way of asserting their independence and autonomy.* This is an example of men's arrested development in adolescence. Remember when your mother would say that you should wear the red jumper instead of the black pants and you'd immediately put on the black pants just to annoy her? Most women have grown out of this rebellious behavior. Unfortunately, lots of men are still there.

Men may also break their promises because they didn't mean them in the first place. This is a way of acting out. Obviously it would be preferable if our partners were straightforward and could just say no instead of agreeing to something and then capitulating because they resent having said yes. This happens quite regularly. For example, you ask him to clean up the basement; he doesn't want to clean up the basement. After you've asked seventeen times, he says, "Fine, I'll clean up the basement." Three weeks later, as you try to get to the washing machine, you're still stumbling over piles of his papers, books, and clothing strewn all over the basement. If he was really honest, he'd say, " 'You know, I shouldn't have agreed to clean the basement because I don't care about the mess' or 'I don't have time' or 'It doesn't matter to me' or . . ." On the other hand, if he wants to please you, he may promise to do something he'd rather not, but then he'll genuinely forget about it (since it doesn't matter to him) or he'll do it if and only if you stand over him with a whip.

Great. Just the position we want to be in: the demanding, nagging woman forcing the poor, beleaguered man to have to take responsibility for things that he'd rather avoid. Yet another impossible setup: We're the bad guy, he's the victim.

At first glance, this seems like an unsolvable problem. It appears as if you have only two lousy options: Stop asking and expecting him to make promises he can't or won't keep. Or keep asking for what you want, at the risk of being disappointed time and time again.

Don't despair. You have other alternatives, which we'll explore in Simple Solutions. But before we tackle them, let's take a look at how you may play a part in creating and maintaining this dynamic.

HOW WE MAKE IT WORSE

This is one of those damned-if-we-do, damned-if-we-don't dilemmas, which may make it somewhat difficult to understand how we may be contributing to the problem. Here's the deal: We want and expect our partner to make certain changes (usually appropriately so), but if we push him, there's a good chance he'll say okay and then break his promises. If we back off and don't ask for what we want, nothing will change, which is a real Catch-22.

We help set up the Catch-22 by trying to get our mate to make promises he'd rather not make. We want him to agree to be more emotionally available, but it's really not his style, and frankly, he'd rather have us back off. Or we want him to promise to clean out the garage or mow the lawn or put the kids in their pajamas, none of which he wants to do, which usually results in his acting out in one way or another. Does this mean we should completely pander to him, never asking our partner to stretch beyond his comfort zone? No. But we do need to take responsibility for the fact that we're the one who is asking, sometimes even pressuring, our mate to make a commitment that he genuinely doesn't want to make.

This is complicated by our struggle to figure out what's appropriate to expect. Now, each of us could easily make a list of "things men should obviously do, without us having to push them, remind them, or reward them," but none of these lists mean a thing. Remember: "Should's" are useless. The only worthwhile way to determine appropriate expectations is by honestly appraising what's possible to attain with the particular man in your life. One man may quickly agree to do the dishes but refuse to consider how his workaholism is affecting your relationship, while another man may be more than willing to cut back hours at work but resists taking on any more household tasks. When we expect more from our mate than is realistic, based on our extensive experience, we end up putting him in a position where he's likely to fail, and putting ourselves in a position where we're bound to be disappointed.

We also just don't know when to give up. I greatly admire women's persistence in trying to improve their relationships, but there's a point at which women ask and ask for the same thing, without seeing any tangible change. Now we're being stupid. If our partner has repeatedly ignored our pleas to spend more time with the family, why would we keep trying and trying to get him to comply? If we've tried dozens of strategies to get him to be more giving, and he still puts himself first 90 percent of the time, we're waging a losing battle, and it's time to retreat. Yes, this means lowering our expectations, but in this case, the alternative is unacceptable. If we keep banging our head against the wall, we're going to get a concussion, and knowing this, we can decide to stop.

We also contribute to the problem by granting him clemency. He breaks a promise, and we forgive him. He falls through on a formal commitment, and we give him yet another chance. We take it upon ourselves to remind him of his promises and reward him lavishly when he comes through.

STOP IT!!! The more we accept his excuses, the less likely he is to be accountable for his actions. We don't have to send him a ten-page contract with all the fine points of our agreement, nor do we need to praise him every time he acts like an adult. Here's what to do instead: Just say what you want and expect your partner either to say yes or no, and if it's yes, hold him to his word.

Holding our partner accountable for his actions is the only way he's going to grow up. And part of taking responsibility means facing the consequences of our actions. But rarely do we follow through on consequences when it comes to our mate. We can pout, threaten, or give him an ultimatum, but these aren't consequences; they're just a way to vent, which is easy for him to dismiss and ignore. Real consequences are related to the behavior; for example, if our mate promises to be home on time for a dinner party and we wait forty-five minutes and then go without him, he has to face the consequences of either not showing up or showing up late and answering to you, his host, and the other people at the party. If we make excuses for him (he had to work late, was stuck in a traffic jam, didn't realize the party started promptly at seven), then he's avoided the consequences and is likely to repeat the same behavior because it hasn't cost him a thing.

Consequences aren't punishment or retribution; they're simply the natural result of certain behavior. If your partner is insensitive to you, the natural consequence is that your feelings are hurt. If he misses his son's Little League game, his son may tell his dad just how disappointed he is. Think of consequences as cause and effect, as the natural result of making certain choices.

So if we're so keen on our partner keeping his promises, why do we sabotage ourselves in some of the aforementioned ways? Why aren't we firmer, tougher, and more realistic in our expectations?

WHAT HOOKS US

It goes back to the fact that we just don't want to give up! We keep wishing, hoping, praying, pushing, convincing, and encouraging our partner to make the changes that are important to us, even when they're difficult or insignificant to him. Letting go feels as if we're throwing in the towel, but that's precisely what we need to do in some cases. Not about everything, but about those changes, promises, and commitments that he makes clear he can't or won't deliver on.

Letting go is tough. It requires us to reconcile the gap between what we want and what we have, between who we wish our partner would be and who he really is. In other words, it takes "getting real," which is the key to the solutions that follow.

SIMPLE SOLUTIONS

The first step is to CHOOSE OUR BATTLES. As in many of the issues in this book, especially those related to wanting our mate to change in one way or another, we need to be really thoughtful in deciding what's worth pushing and what is better left alone.

Knowing your priorities is essential to this process. It's up to you to determine what are bottom-line issues that are critical to address in order to remain in and feel fundamentally satisfied with your relationship, as compared to those issues that you can live with, whether or not he changes.

Priorities range wildly from couple to couple. One woman's most burning issue is her husband's lack of ambition, another bemoans the lack of a sex life, while another longs for her partner to be more affectionate and attentive. Each of us has different issues that make us crazy, and those are the ones to concentrate on when choosing our battles.

Here's a useful exercise: Write down the ten most difficult, pressing, and ongoing issues in your relationship. Now, narrow the list down to five—the five that frustrate you the most and create the most friction between you and your mate. Now choose your top two from the list. These are your most monumental battles and where you should invest your energy. If you want your partner to take you seriously, only bring up these two issues. Again, less is more. If we overwhelm our mate with too much, his circuits get overloaded and he tunes us out. If, however, we only bring up one or two truly significant issues, he's more likely to perceive the gravity of the situation and respond in a serious way.

The second strategy involves your being a bit emotionally detached. I'm not suggesting you try not to take your partner's response personally, but it's important to SEPARATE YOUR FEELINGS FROM HIS BEHAVIOR. In other words, we have to make a concerted effort not to interpret his actions as symbolic, as a reflection of his commitment or love. This is difficult. If we tell our partner it's terribly important to us that he notice how we look and he never says a word, it's hard not to interpret it as meaning he is either deaf, dumb, or just doesn't care. Likewise, if we've made it perfectly clear that we desperately want our mate to quit making sarcastic wisecracks about us and he continues, naturally we feel that if he "really loved us" he wouldn't act like an insensitive brute. I realize this is a stretch, but men's behavior isn't usually as symbolic as we make it out to be. (This is one of the reasons so many men tell women to take them at face value instead of psychoanalyzing their secret motivations.)

Believe him! He may continually ignore your request for him to notice your appearance, but it may not be for the reason you think. He may be distracted, he may be unattracted (which is another problem in and of itself), or it may not occur to him, forget that you've asked dozens of times. I can think of a handful of conversations I've had with boyfriends or lovers who, when I said, "I wish you'd comment on how nice I look, or notice that I got all dressed up for you," respond with genuine surprise that I wouldn't just know that they think I'm gorgeous and sexy. (Excuse me, but did they totally miss that long conversation we had when I confided about having been a fat, ugly kid?) At any rate, if you can, avoid putting too much meaning into your partner's actions, because they may not mean what you think.

In terms of chronic promise breaking, one simple strategy is to STOP ASKING YOUR PARTNER TO MAKE PROMISES. Promises are intimidating; they carry a lot of weight and consequently create greater feelings of pressure. No one wants to make a promise they can't keep, and when your partner finds himself in that uncomfortable position, that's where some of the trouble starts.

An alternative is to ENCOURAGE YOUR PARTNER TO MAKE

AN EFFORT. Emphasize the value of "trying" rather than making promises he might not be able to keep. Trying is what you're really after, anyway. If you can reward effort as much or more than outcome, you'll reduce the pressure, increase his chance of performing successfully, and be happier with the result.

When he does make a promise, however, HOLD HIM TO HIS WORD! Don't pussyfoot around in order to avoid an argument or salvage his ego. This is a form of "enabling"—what's known in the codependence field as supporting and reinforcing our partner's negative behavior out of fear or need for his love and approval. Every time we look the other way or give him one more chance we give him the message that there's no real consequences for his actions, in which case, there's no real reason for him to change. Again, consequences aren't a form of punishment or blame; they're simply the natural outcome of making certain choices. If he hurts you, tell him. If he lets you down let him know you're disappointed. If he breaks a promise, make sure he knows he's diminished your trust. This is a case of what he doesn't know will hurt him. Just as it's hard to make our children face up to their mistakes, it's painful (although sometimes it's pleasurable—just deserts) to follow through on consequences with our mate. But it's the only way they learn—and the only way any lasting change occurs.

Ultimately, the best way to avoid getting hurt over broken promises is to WATCH WHAT HE DOES INSTEAD OF LISTENING TO WHAT HE SAYS. I don't know about you, but I'm a sucker for a man staring deeply in my eyes, apologizing for hurting me, and promising he'll never ever do it again. I melt every time—until I get burned.

Behavior is all that counts. Your partner can promise

you the moon, but if his best shot is a patch of grass in the backyard, then that's what's real and that's what's worth getting invested in. In other words, GET WHAT'S POSSIBLE, WORK WITHIN REASON TOWARD TRYING TO GET HIM TO MAKE BOTTOM-LINE CHANGES, AND ACCEPT THE FACT THAT THERE WILL ALWAYS BE A GAP BETWEEN WHAT YOU WANT AND WHAT YOU GET. As long as you keep getting a little more of what you want, you're in pretty good shape.

ON THE BRIGHT SIDE

It's a great relief to choose our battles and let go of some of our more unrealistic expectations and less crucial issues. We recover some of the life energy we are expending trying to get blood from a stone, energy that we can refocus in more productive ways. We are also able to focus on the most important issues instead of spinning our wheels trying to do a complete overhaul.

It's very liberating to let go of some of the struggle. Even if everything isn't perfect, or even close, the more we are able to accept and/or moderate our urgency at getting our mate to change, the happier we'll be and the more gratitude we'll feel for what's good and right in our relationship. Now wouldn't that be nice for a change?

14

If he doesn't treat you well

━━━━◆━━━━

This chapter title needs some explanation: By "doesn't treat you well" I'm not referring to any level of physical abuse. That's patently unacceptable. Assuming this isn't true of your relationship, I've intentionally included a variety of issues under the umbrella of our partner treating us badly. There are many different manifestations of this, including:

- CRITICIZING YOU, especially in public
- BEING DISLOYAL by not standing up for you in front of family or friends
- HURTING YOUR FEELINGS by being crass or insensitive
- MAKING NEGATIVE COMMENTS (or no comment) about your appearance
- BEING A BULLY by screaming, yelling, or verbally intimidating you

- ACTING SARCASTIC by being caustic or cutting and then saying, "Oh honey, I was just kidding"
- RETALIATING by using personal information you've shared to shame you or make you feel bad about yourself
- BEING NEGLECTFUL by avoiding you or acting as if you don't exist

It's a long list, and it's only a brief compilation of some of the most universal ways in which men are mean to their mates. Of course, what hurts one woman doesn't necessarily hurt another; one man's worst mistake can be another man's finest moment, depending on the relationship.

By way of illustration, several years ago a woman I know was given sexy black lingerie as a birthday gift from her husband. I don't think he meant to hurt her. In fact, I expect he was excited (in several ways) to give it to her and was shocked by her reaction. This woman, who'd battled her weight for years, found this choice of gift deeply hurtful and insensitive. She took it as making one of any number of possible negative statements, including: her husband was oblivious to where she was at emotionally; he was making fun of her; he wanted to humiliate her. In any case, she threw the lingerie in his face and went to bed in tears.

I, on the other hand, die for men to give me the sexist, barest, most revealing lingerie they can buy without blushing. No longer a fat ugly girl (in my head or in reality), I love my body and enjoy prancing around in black lace.

But that's me. And that's the point. When our partner knows something will hurt us, why would he do it? Why would someone who says he loves us intentionally treat us poorly?

The key element is *intention.* Hurtful acts aren't always intentional. Sometimes our partner may do something mean or nasty without having any desire to hurt us. This certainly isn't limited to men; all of us, women and men alike, say or do the wrong thing without any intent to harm another person. We may be crabby, self-absorbed, or even insensitive, but we're not being malicious. While it still hurts, it's much easier to forgive someone for being moody or oblivious than for being outright hateful and purposefully going out of their way to hurt us.

Of course, the defense "I didn't mean to hurt you" may just be an easy way out, especially since our partners have a pretty good idea of how to injure us. It's what we mean when we say "You're pushing my buttons"—based on experience, you know exactly my vulnerabilities, and you're intentionally attacking me in a weak place.

In her book *Beyond Codependency,* author Melody Beatty says, "Of course your parents know how to push your buttons. Who do you think installed them?" The same is true, to a lesser extent, with our romantic partners. Especially those of us who have been with the same person for years and are well aware of what buttons to push to get a rise out of our partner. Here, being "mean" is demonstrated as manipulation; when we know how to hurt our partner—and actively choose to do so—that's a fairly serious offense.

When our partner treats us poorly, either by being critical, insulting, or neglectful, we feel betrayed. We recoil in hurt, anger, and shock, sometimes to the point of outrage, that our partner could treat us so poorly. Our first response is likely to be, "You love me? You sure aren't acting like it!"

For the fifth or sixth time, I repeat: When our partner hurts us, it's not necessarily because he doesn't love us. He may not be acting in a loving manner, but what he's expressing is that he's basically out of control rather than his lack of commitment. There are, of course, incidents in which our mate may be mean as a way to push us away because he's actually unhappy in our relationship. This is the "I'll be so crappy to you, you'll be dying to leave me, so I won't have to be the one to say it's over." This is the most extreme case, which we'll explore a bit further on in the chapter.

Whatever his motivation, it's essential to know that you *don't deserve to be treated poorly.* You may have done something to upset or enrage your partner, but this still doesn't entitle him to mistreat you. Once again, it would be easier to just conclude that men are jerks, and leave it at that. But it wouldn't be telling the whole story, or even the central plot. The fact is, when men are hurtful it's for a reason, and assuming your mate isn't an abusive jerk, there are other, deeper explanations for his behavior.

WHY ARE THEY LIKE THIS?

I'm still somewhat of a self-help aficionada, influenced by the "inner child" "wounded soul" perspectives of the late nineties. I do believe that most of us have sustained some emotional scars as a result of our upbringing, and that when these wounds aren't healed, we tend to act them out in our relationships.

Without retracting what I said in my introduction—that

there's a point at which it's time to grow up and get beyond our childhood traumas—it simply follows that some of men's worst behavior is traceable to their childhood wounds. In short, *they hurt us because they've been hurt.* Any of us who haven't dealt with our unfinished business inevitably bring the remnants into our relationship. Men are especially prone to be hurtful as an unconscious alternative to honestly expressing their feelings. When they can't identify or name what's really going on, they're apt to inappropriately let out their sadness, anger, or hurt. The unexamined psyche is a dangerous weapon, one used both to hurt us and to hurt others. If your mate hasn't ever taken an honest look at himself, expressed legitimate rage, and shed real tears, he's more likely to express his unhealed hurt in hurtful ways, most often toward his partner.

Ironically, we tend to "hurt the ones we love" because with them we feel safest to be our worst selves. I saw this recently with my children. For a few weeks, both of my normally nice kids had been mean and snotty toward me. I tried my usual tactic: First, I tried getting them to tell me what was really going on. Then I tried being empathetic, then being distant and trying not to take it to heart. I talked to a few parents of teenagers, who reassured me that this was perfectly age-appropriate behavior before wishing me good luck and promising that my kids would be lovable in about eight years. Then something happened that reminded me of how and why we tend to be hurtful to those we love and trust the most. Each of my children, independently, told me that the reason they could be mean to me was because they "knew that I would always love them, no matter what."

Those of us who are mothers agree that this is absolutely true, which of course doesn't excuse our kids from being, at minimum, disrespectful. Whereas we may not love our mate that unconditionally, part of the reason we are his target is based on his confidence that our love is solid enough to survive his poor behavior.

He may also be mean because he feels that you've been mean to him. Now before you go defending yourself, relationships are a two-way street, and whether you have actually hurt him or he just thinks so, he may be striking back in defense. C'mon! We aren't perfect angels, but we certainly aren't at fault each time our partner is a jerk; there are plenty of times he's been mean when we've been perfectly nice. Sad to say, at times we are victimized by our partners, and if this happens repeatedly, we need to seek a good therapist and do some serious thinking about whether we belong in this relationship.

But most women's partners aren't that hurtful or harmful. More often, the "hurts" in our relationship are infrequent but painful enough for us to wince, cry out, or pull back in order to protect ourselves. One way to protect ourselves is to honestly explore how we may aggravate the problem.

HOW WE MAKE IT WORSE

We aren't immune from childhood wounds, either. Not always, but at times, we may anger our partner by provoking, taunting, criticizing, or putting him down. Often we hurt one another in a tag-you're-it kind of way. What starts out as a fairly decent conversation turns into verbal Ping-Pong; before we know it, we are slinging insults until it escalates to all-out war. If one of us has felt hurt and hasn't mentioned it, it's common to be sideswiped by anger that's so buried or repressed we're unaware of it. That's when we say and do some of the meanest things. We let down our inhibitions in a barrage of insults and criticism we would normally control. Given the degree of past hurt many of us have received from our mate, it's fair to assume that we may, at times, react by being mean and vindictive.

Not to beat a dead horse, but we may also not be so fabulous to live with, between our cumulative anger and our level of stress. We may blame our mate for being the source of our unhappiness, we may accuse him of any number of infractions, slight or serious, and we may just be bitchy because we're tired, overwhelmed, PMS-y, or having a lousy day. This is simply to point out that when our mate is mean, he may be reacting to how we are treating him.

But as often as we may go on the offensive, we're still far more likely to allow ourselves to be treated like victims. I'm waiting for the day when no books will be written for women telling us how to stop letting ourselves be hurt. Far too often—in fact, anytime is one time too many—we take our mate's insults, criticism, or abuse without defending ourselves and without letting him know how furious we are.

We let an awful lot pass, for a number of different reasons. We may be scared that fighting back will further provoke our mate. We may feel so dependent on him we are afraid to stand up for our rights. We may believe that we provoked our mate's behavior and therefore deserve to be punished. And we may be so scared of losing our relationship that we're willing to put up with being treated badly rather than being alone.

There is no excuse for letting ourselves be victimized!

Dramatic statistics reveal that thousands, maybe hundreds of thousands, of women are physically abused by their partners and remain silent rather than calling the police or going to a shelter. In a way, we are doing the same thing when we allow our partner to be mean or nasty, and either ignore it, pacify him, or cry in the bathroom alone.

I applaud women who refuse to put up with disrespectful behavior, and there are plenty of them out there. I'm particularly impressed by my teenaged daughter, Zoe, and her friends. They have an "I don't take shit from anyone" attitude, which is largely influenced by their role models, like Ani DiFranco and Alanis Morissette. I say, Go girls!

But those of us who are intimidated, too scared, or too "nice" to fight back or defend ourselves, aren't doing ourselves or our partner any favors. I'm certainly one of them. It's taken me until my early forties to actually get angry with a man. I mean steaming, screaming mad, and believe me, he deserved it. Up until now, my response to being hurt has been to get sad instead of getting mad. When we don't get angry over things that we should be angry at, we turn our feelings inward, which often results in depression, which has hit frightening heights in the past decade. Why do we have such a hard time getting angry when it's totally appropriate?

WHAT HOOKS US

All we want is for things to be nice between us, for our relationship to be a loving, supportive sanctuary. We may allow our mate to treat us poorly because we are so totally invested in our relationship. We don't want to lose him, so we tolerate intolerable behavior so as not to rock the boat.

We may also get hooked if our partner actually acknowledges that he's hurt us but defends his behavior with two words that men seem to think are sufficient to justify their actions: "I'm scared." To be fair, we've had a part in giving men the message that this is not only an acceptable excuse but deserving of our sympathy and forgiveness. But it no longer works. (Maybe it just got used once too often, but plenty of women are sick of this answer. Instead of invoking our compassion, it's more likely to make us think or say something like "Get over it" or "So what? You're scared, I'm scared, but that doesn't give you the right to ball." This is a step in the right direction. Change only occurs when we hold men accountable for their actions, regardless of how scared they may be.

We may also be so accustomed to being treated poorly that we don't even notice it anymore. He's been badgering us for so many years, we tune him out or pass it off as another one of "Henry's moods." Or we are so used to his temper tantrums, we excuse them as stress or just his personality, which we've learned to live with. This is called "being in denial," contemporary lingo for pretending something isn't happening because it hurts too much to face it.

We may also be numb. After years of cumulative wounds, we may be somewhat impervious to our partner's ill behavior. Each hurt causes another new scab to form over the wound, until we can't even feel the original pain. Actually, we can't afford to feel the pain, so we convince ourselves it actually doesn't hurt.

But it does. And it's unacceptable, for our own health and well-being, as well as for the long-term success of our relationship. The truth is, no one wants to be mean. We and our partners ultimately want the same thing: to get along and have a peaceful, loving relationship. Given this, how do we deal with our mate treating us badly? And how do we keep from hurting him back?

SIMPLE SOLUTIONS

First and foremost, TELL HIM WHEN HE'S TREATING YOU BADLY! Don't turn the other cheek and don't make excuses to yourself. Remember: You never deserve to be mistreated, and the only way to stop it is by calling it to your partner's attention and insisting he hear you out.

Now, you needn't start with accusations. The sure way for a fight to escalate is by beginning with blame rather than by giving him the benefit of the doubt. Remember our conversation about intentions? A good way to start is by investigating his motives. In other words, ASK HIM WHAT'S GOING ON.

This doesn't mean you have to act like his therapist instead of his mistreated mate. It just means ask. Ask him why he just blew up when all you did was ask him to pass the salt. Ask him why he's being cold to you for no apparent reason. Ask him why he's being critical of you when you just told him you're feeling insecure. Ask. Ask. Ask.

Depending on his answer, decide how you intend to respond. You have lots of choices, but all of them require telling him that he's hurt you. You can be very specific and just say, "It hurt me that you ignored me most of the evening when we were having dinner with the Smiths." (It's always wise to attach behavior to feelings, in other words, instead of just saying "You hurt me," say "This particular behavior of yours was hurtful."

Examples are powerful; they help us to express why

we're hurt, and they make it hard for our partner either to plead innocence or come up with some half-assed explanation. Here are some other good choices: You can Retreat Until You're Ready to Deal with Him. (Sometimes a little perspective helps us sort out our feelings and figure out the most productive way to proceed.) You can pout until he asks what's wrong. (It's a little retrograde, but it works.) You can go at it full force, venting your rage and giving it to him so that there's no mistaking that his behavior is patently unacceptable. (This one's dramatic, but the downside is the possibility of increasing his rage.) And you can simply say, "Please stop hurting me. It's not okay."

There's something to be said for taking the higher ground, although with repeated incidents being nice falls on deaf ears. If you can state your feelings calmly, letting him know exactly how you feel, that's your best chance of getting a positive result.

What's a positive result? Ideally, our partner apologizes, means it, and makes a genuine commitment to clean up his act. That's the best-case scenario. More typically, he may retreat in shame or retaliate, however weak his position. For this reason, it helps for us to know what we need him to do to make it better. We may need to hear him say "I'm sorry." We may need to watch him squirm. We may need to let some time pass before we stop being sore. But usually what we need is for our feelings to be acknowledged and some evidence that change is occurring.

Again, Watch the Behavior. Our perceptions only shift when we have a new and different experience. If we've spent years tolerating our mate's irrational outbursts, cutting sarcasm or demeaning comments, it may take several months of the absence of this behavior for us to begin to trust him. Trust can be regained and forgiveness can be granted, but not until we have tangible evidence that we can expect improved behavior.

Meanwhile, you need to KNOW HOW TO PROTECT YOURSELF. It's a shame that we have to erect a protective shield with the one person whom we should be able to trust the most. But in all relationships, this is fairly unavoidable to some degree or another. It's the rare couple who sustains a relationship without experiencing a certain amount of hurt. With time, hopefully, we learn how to be more loving. But until then, we have to develop ways to keep ourselves emotionally safe.

Some women protect themselves by walking away—not out of the relationship, but out of the room, or out of the house, until they're ready to reengage. Other women protect themselves by emotionally withdrawing in one way or another; we may be altogether present in our relationship while not being entirely emotionally available, which is just fine. Trust is earned, and sometimes it has to be earned over and over. Other women set up a barrier, sometimes even a brick wall, to protect them from getting hurt. Their embitterment has grown to the point at which they're no longer willing to let their partner in. This is the most dangerous scenario, in that the higher the wall the more estranged we become, and the less we are able to improve our relationship.

If this describes you, think hard and long about what it would take to forgive your mate. If you are unable to come up with an answer, a skilled therapist can help you understand your pain and figure out what it would take for you to forgive your partner and begin anew. Be aware that you may not want to forgive him. There's a certain satisfaction in being right, in being the wounded party, but ultimately, this is just another defense mechanism, which won't, in the long haul, give you the love and reconciliation you really want.

I trust that's what most of us want. Obviously, we have only limited control over our partner's behavior. He may continue to act like a jerk at times, when we've done nothing to provoke him and have nothing to do with his behavior. At these times, whenever possible, it helps to repeat to ourselves: "This is not about me." We still get the brunt of his anger, but at least we know we're not responsible for his behavior. And that's the best way to counteract this issue. Regardless of how he treats us, we can take comfort in knowing that we are being our best selves in our relationship, which we must continue to do as long as we choose to be with our mate. A reminder: You chose him. And at present, you're still choosing him. As long as you choose to be with him, when he's shitty, call him on it; when you're hurt, tell him. But regardless of his actions, don't sink to his level. Keep being someone you can be proud of.

ON THE BRIGHT SIDE

It can only get better. Sorry, that's the best I can do. The only conceivable positive aspect to your partner being mean to you is his learning to stop. And now you have the tools to help him and to help yourself. Plus, you have a few extra advantages: You won't allow yourself to be victimized ever again. You won't turn your anger inward, and you will know how to better protect yourself. And you'll keep cultivating your own integrity, which will serve you in your relationship, or in another relationship, if that's what the future holds.

If he doesn't make your relationship enough of a priority

One final complaint: Why do so many women feel as if their partner isn't as committed as they are to their relationship?

"We have a really good marriage except that Reid doesn't care about our relationship as much as I do," says Kathy, who's been married for six years. "For example, he hardly ever comes up with fun or romantic things for us to do. He doesn't help with the kids. He avoids dealing with our issues. He hardly ever touches me except when he wants sex. I have to send him memos to remind him it's our anniversary, he refuses to make any plans for the future . . ."

Whoa! After listening to Kathy and numerous other women expressing similar sentiments, I'm convinced that this issue belongs in this book. In fact, it may actually be at the crux of the so-called battle of the sexes, the bedrock issue from which many if not most problems arise.

The feeling or belief that we care more about our relationships than our partner does is a typical complaint among women. But how it's experienced and expressed takes a great variety of forms. For instance, Nan resents that her husband, David, shoots hoops with his male friends three nights a week instead of spending at least one or two of his free nights with her. Anne is upset that her husband, Peter, refuses to even talk about the possibility of having a second child. Lynn complains that her boyfriend, Marty, who she's been dating exclusively for six months, still hasn't introduced her to his family. And sometimes it's just a nagging feeling that somehow, in some abstract, intangible way, our partner doesn't put the same value and importance on our relationship that we do.

You're right. He doesn't. Not to say that he's apathetic or halfway out the door. Not even close! He may cherish you, be extremely committed to your relationship, and still not place an equal priority on it, at least in ways that matter to you.

Since we're covering a lot of ground here, for the sake of brevity and clarity, let's narrow this issue down. Let's call it: Women who put their relationship at the top, or near the top, of their list of priorities and men who value their relationship, but not necessarily more than their work, their car, their friendships, or other aspects of their lives.

Now we're really back to the reality that he's a guy, which we may as well accept if we're to get anywhere, especially on this topic. Being a guy, in this case, means some of his values, priorities, and how they're both demonstrated, is notably different from ours. In other words, he's not a woman and he's not going to act like one.

How are we different? We have numerous pressing pri-

ELLEN SUE STERN

orities—our career, our friendships, our political concerns—but our relationship comes first, challenged only by our commitment to our kids. Our partner, on the other hand, doesn't necessarily see our relationship as the most central commitment in his life. Two other concrete examples: We want to know everything about him; he wants to know certain parts of us. Or we want other priorities to be secondary to or arranged around our relationship, whereas he may make other choices, leaving our relationship to get the leftovers of his attention and energy.

More exceptions to the rule. I know several men who consistently put their relationship first, who go out of their way to surprise their partner with thoughtful gifts, make romantic weekend plans, and set aside time to really talk, even if they've brought work home or are dying to watch their favorite *Star Trek* rerun. A recent cultural phenomenon, the Promise Keepers (I'm neither advocating nor criticizing this movement), which is an organization of Christian men whose alleged mission is to make their family the main priority in their lives, is another example of men starting to shift their attention from worldly concerns to the realm of love and intimacy.

Still, the majority of women feel some inequity between how much their relationship matters to them versus where it falls in their partner's priorities. This doesn't have to be a problem! We can both bridge the gap and learn to accept the differences, but as long as it creates distress in our relationship, it makes sense to explore this issue and find ways to improve it.

Exploring the underlying reasons for men's behavior in this arena can help unlock the key to approaching this issue in a positive and productive spirit. First, let's look

222

at why men don't necessarily value their relationship the way we do.

WHY ARE THEY LIKE THIS?

Let's review our earlier conversation about how girls are brought up to prize personal relationships, whereas *boys are raised to prize autonomy.* Remember that most of our male partners were brought up to have far less interest and investment in romance and intimacy. We played with Barbie dolls, orchestrating lavish weddings to Ken, devoured articles in teen magazines on flirting techniques and flattering outfits, and spent much of our teenage and young-adult years focused on finding a man whom we could love and cherish "till death do us part."

Trust me, our male counterparts weren't even thinking about things like this, much less spending their time wondering, worrying, or strategizing how to create the perfect relationship. They were playing football, collecting stamps, working on their cars, and thinking about what they'd be when they grew up, not who they'd fall in love with and/ or marry. Now, naturally, they were thinking about sex. But that's different from intimacy, and certainly a far shot from emotional commitment. And we, of course, weren't only thinking about boys. We, too, were serious about our education, friendships, and other extracurricular activities, but boys were always at the forefront of our minds.

I'm not sure things have changed all that much in this category. While my daughter, Zoe, has a part-time job, is an aspiring writer, a member of the National Youth AIDS Counsel, Young Judea, and plans on playing lacrosse this spring, I venture to say most of her waking hours are still spent thinking about and talking to boys. The majority of her conversation revolves around who's going with whom and who's broken up with whom, and hours are spent on the phone either talking to boys or talking about them to her friends. In contrast, although my son, Evan, is just thirteen, while he's clearly interested in girls, they're hardly what he lives for. He's at least as interested in playing soccer, logging onto the Internet, or hanging out with his buddies as he is in worrying about whether or not he has a girlfriend.

Besides not focusing solely on females, *men are brought up to be more diversified than women.* Our partners were most likely encouraged and reinforced for being involved in a variety of activities, be it athletics, the school newspaper, religious youth groups, or just hanging out with the guys. In contrast, girls were kept a little closer to home; our activities were generally more supervised, and we were less likely to be urged to get involved in lots of extracurricular activities, unless they related to academics, homemaking, or social functions designed to promote heterosexual relationships. When I was growing up, being a cheerleader was coveted, but girls' athletic activities were virtually nonexistent. Consequently many women have had to push themselves—and make a concerted effort to encourage their daughters—to expand their horizons and pursue their interests, passions, and dreams, instead of being overly focused on the man in our life.

Second, it's true that men don't need women as much as women need men. Or, at least, *men don't think they need us as much as we need them, and certainly not in the same ways.* In fact, we know better. Watch one man go to pieces when the love of his life sends him a Dear John letter and "macho men" images will fly right out the window. This is particularly true on a practical level, as is evidenced by how utterly helpless widowers are when their spouse dies. They can't even open a can of tuna, much less make dinner plans to ease their loneliness, which is why they're prime bait for widows or single women who want to date or get married. Once a man has had a woman in his life, he has an incredibly hard time being alone.

Our partner may also downplay the importance of our relationship because it presents too much conflict or too many challenges. Being with us can be wonderful, but just as often it can be problematic, especially when we're confronting him on difficult issues. Face it: Guys just wanna have fun. The guy who is a workaholic knows what's expected of him and feels confident of and competent in his ability to perform. In short, men may put more energy into anything but our relationship because other things are simply more enjoyable. More satisfying. Or less potentially difficult, and remember, *men avoid conflict at all costs.*

Our mates may also communicate how much they value our relationship in ways that we don't recognize. As Jerry, one of my clients, remarked during a therapy session, "I don't know what Tina's talking about. I don't go out at night with the guys, I spend every weekend with her, and whenever she says, 'You don't really love me,' I always say, 'I'm still here, aren't I?'"

Bad answer! I'd like to give men a list of good responses and bad responses. As often as not, a man puts his foot in his mouth by saying exactly the opposite of what his partner wants to hear. For example, "I'm still here, aren't I?" gets a D–, whereas "You're the most precious thing in my life" gets an A. Likewise, "Yeah, you do look like you've put on a little weight" (even if she's asked, "Do you think I look fat?) are words that should never pass through a man's lips. I don't care if she's gained twenty pounds, the only right answer is: "Honey, you look beautiful."

If it sounds as if I'm encouraging men to coddle women, I am. And they should. There's a fine line between telling the truth, however harsh and painful, and choosing our words carefully so as not to hurt the one we love. As we've discussed throughout this book, men will often withdraw from our relationship if they sense the possibility of conflict, and their seeming inability to make the relationship a priority is yet another example of behavior that is uniquely male. If they feel that their method of expressing their love and commitment is inadequate or unappreciated, they're likely to put less and less energy into maintaining the relationship.

We, too, play a role in this dynamic, which we will examine now.

HOW WE MAKE IT WORSE

For starters, women need to put a little less emphasis on our love relationship whereas men need to put a little bit more. This same formula operates in a number of areas; for instance, we need to do less, and he needs to do more. We need to have a bit more emotional restraint; he could be a bit more forthcoming.

In other words, *we need to need him less.* The truth is, we can say that men don't care about our relationship as much as we do, but it's equally true that we may put a little too much of our energy into making our partner so central in our lives.

This has been an ongoing fight between my last boyfriend and myself. He accuses me of being overly invested in our relationship (that is, you need me too much), and I accuse him of not being invested enough (that is, you don't really love me). It's a futile argument and an unproductive power struggle. When accused of wanting or needing our relationship to be more of a priority, I'd feel embarrassed and vulnerable. I'd immediately start defending myself, reminding him that "besides you, I have two kids, an extremely demanding career, twenty-five close friends, two cats, an extended family, not to mention numerous community involvements, so don't flatter yourself!"

Clearly we're not obsessed with our relationship; we may just need to make it slightly less central to our existence. Doing this narrows the gap between how important he sees the relationship versus what priority it plays in our lives. This isn't to say that we should stop caring deeply about our relationship and investing in it, mind, heart, and soul. *We simply need to balance our level of commitment with other, equally important and nurturing aspects of our lives.* Otherwise we end up feeling overly needy and resenting his apparent lack of equal involvement.

One strategic mistake we make is confronting or pushing our partner to prove his devotion. Yet another setup. Testing our partner by demanding that he demonstrate greater commitment is sure to make him feel pressured and even less willing to put our relationship first. *No one likes to be tested;* he'll resent it, and besides, nothing he says or does will actually convince us that he's really "in" our relationship in the way we want.

We're far better off to modify our expectations and to whatever degree possible accept and appreciate the ways in which our partner expresses his devotion. But before we move on to strategies, it's useful to understand what makes us so bent out of shape when our partner doesn't seem to value our relationship the way we do.

WHAT HOOKS US

Most women are hopeless romantics. Obviously, there are tough, hardcore I-can-live-with-him-or-without-him types, but for the most part we are softies when it comes to love. Our hearts melt when our partner shows up with flowers or spontaneously says, "God, I'm the luckiest man in the world."

It comes down to this: We want him. We want all of him. *We want to feel as if we're the most treasured person in his life,* and when we don't get that message, we feel rejected and alone in our relationship. We yearn for our partner to be our best friend, our most trusted confidant, and our relationship to be a holy sanctuary in which each of us is equally invested. All of this is wonderful to want. Without women's efforts, love relationships wouldn't have the level of intimacy and communion we yearn for. So thank goodness for women. But meanwhile, we're still stuck, if you will, with men who may neither share nor express our priorities the way we do. Given this disparity, how do we narrow the gap? What simple steps can we take either to increase our partner's overt commitment or accept that we may have qualitatively different stakes in our relationship?

SIMPLE SOLUTIONS

Guess what? We're back to the same old thing: We have to ask for what we want in order to facilitate change in our relationship. In this case, we need to ask our partner for specific behavioral changes that will reassure us that our relationship is as important to him as it is to us.

It may be hard to pinpoint what to ask for. The best way to figure this out is to MAKE A WRITTEN LIST OF WHAT'S MISSING IN YOUR RELATIONSHIP. For example, if you are frustrated that your partner "never" (in quotes, because *never* is often an exaggeration of reality) makes a big deal of your birthday or anniversary, then put it on your list. If he doesn't pay enough attention to you, put it on your list. If he fills up his calendar so that there's little time for the two of you or if he refuses to make mutual plans for the future, put it on your list.

Your list reveals what you want from your partner in order to believe that he sees your relationship as a high priority. Once you make your list, as always, when you approach your mate, be nice, be polite, and be specific. Don't throw a fit, accusing him of not knowing or caring if you're alive, and don't succumb to slamming, criticizing, or shaming him. And above all else, give him a way to improve by presenting him with concrete ways he can demonstrate his commitment.

Second, BE SURE TO NOTICE, ACKNOWLEDGE, AND RE-WARD ANY AND ALL WAYS IN WHICH YOUR MATE EXPRESSES HIS DEVOTION. Remember: We express commitment in different ways. You may want romantic gestures, while he's out getting the oil in your car changed—his way of manifesting his involvement. He's spent the weekend painting the basement, and you're mad that he hasn't had time to spend a leisurely Sunday at the lake with you and the kids. It's human nature to interpret other's actions on the basis of what we would mean if we were to do the same thing, but it doesn't work that way. For example, our husband may be excited to give us a new microwave oven or portable phone for Christmas, which disappoints us, since we were hoping for the tennis bracelet we circled in the newspaper and left on his pillow.

The truth is, we give what we want to get. And we show our love in the way that we want to be loved, rather than paying attention to what speaks to and pleases our partner, even if it's dramatically different from what would please us. This is one of the fundamental truths of human nature—and it's important to understand in this context. Why? Because one of the simplest solutions is to focus on appreciating the unique ways in which our mate actively shows his devotion, which may change our feeling that we care more about the relationship than he does. If we're really open-minded, we may be pleasantly surprised to see how much he truly expresses his commitment.

The third simple strategy is to MAKE YOUR RELATIONSHIP MORE FUN! Seriously! As I stated in the introduction to this book, our relationships have become too much work and not nearly enjoyable enough. There will always be issues, conflicts, and challenges to meet in our relationship, but we needn't solely or mostly focus on that aspect of our relationship.

Everything in moderation. If we put half our emotional intensity into having fun with our mate instead of trying to get him to change, he'd be more available, we'd get more of what we want, and our relationship would prosper. There's a direct ratio between fun in a relationship and the amount of stress and conflict it can endure. Here's another area in which you have more power than you think. At least a few times a week, set aside any grievances or heavy conversations and plan something fun to do with your mate. A drive-in movie. A picnic. Several uninterrupted hours in bed. If you make your relationship more fun then your partner is guaranteed to be more interested in nurturing and putting his best energy into it.

To repeat: Don't Make Your Relationship Your Primary Purpose and Meaning in Life. Expanding your investments, whether by getting more involved in your work, spending more time with your children, parents, or friends, or pursuing interests that stimulate and strengthen you are the best ways to counter feelings of insecurity related to feeling more involved than your mate. The fuller your life, the less dependent you are on him. And the less dependent you are on him, the more forthcoming he'll be. It works like a charm. Don't do it as a manipulation, do it to enhance your level of personal happiness and fulfillment. Remember, every strategy in this book is meant to improve your life, whether or not it improves your relationship.

By all means, keep loving your partner and letting him know how dear and important he is to you. Give according to your genuine feelings of love, and it won't matter as much whether he gives back in time. Loving is at least as gratifying as being loved. Sometimes more so.

ON THE BRIGHT SIDE

There are three potential rewards for trying the simple solutions I've discussed. First, you get to feel how deeply devoted you are to your partner, which is a real plus, especially if you've been having doubts about your relationship. Second, by listening to your feelings and requests, your mate has the chance to express his commitment in a way that will convince you he's the real thing. Lastly, you'll gain inner strength and empowerment by widening your circle of love and support. In other words, there's nothing to lose and everything to gain.

And One for Good Luck: If he doesn't say "I love you" enough

━━━━━━━━━━━━◆━━━━━━━━━━━━

This one's short and sweet. If I could get every couple in America to include three sentences on a regular basis in their relationships, they would be, "I'm sorry," "Thank you," and the most magical words of all, "I love you."

No other words have the same power to heal a relationship and move it forward to a better place. Up until now I've advocated paying attention to what your partner does, not to what he says. This is the exception. I don't want to in any way minimize or diminish the importance of your mate's expressing love to you in actions, but saying the words "I love you" is in a category all by itself. We reserve these words for intimate connections and moments of splendor. We use them sparingly, far too sparingly, if you want my opinion. There are, of course, the token "I love you's" thrown over the shoulder on the way out the door to work or before drifting off to sleep, but those don't count. They're simply part of our routine way of communicating with our mate.

What we are missing are the excruciatingly sweet, deeply felt moments of gratitude when we spontaneously turn to our partner in absolute awe and whisper, "God. I really love you."

These are the moments that make all the rest of it worthwhile—the conflicts, disappointments, frustrations, and feelings of doubt. We need to hear "I love you" often and not just to reassure us that he's still attracted and interested. "I love you," when spoken within the context of an intimate love relationship, says more than that. It says, "I'm so lucky to have you." And, "You're still the one person on the planet with whom I want to spend my life."

"I love you's" get forgotten in the daily clutter of our stressed-out lives. We're so busy making a living, making a home, running kids from one place to the next, that we don't remember how important it is to stop for a moment and overtly express our adoration. We figure there's always later, or tomorrow, or another more convenient time, but that's like buying a lottery ticket and stuffing it in your drawer without bothering to see if the numbers match up. The phrase "No time like the present," applies here in spades. It's naive and arrogant to assume there will be infinite opportunities to say "I love you." *It takes so little and it means so much.* Knowing this, why do we pass up the opportunity to say the three words that can make the most difference in our relationship?

WHY ARE BOTH OF US LIKE THIS?

For the first and only time in this book, we will explore both yours and your partner's motivations together, rather than looking at them separately. Why? Because this is one issue where women and men are equally at fault. I feel safe in saying that we are just as guilty as men when it comes to forgetting to say "I love you," and for the very same reasons.

First, *we simply take one another for granted.* We may think that our partner knows we love him or her (wrong!) without our having to spell it out. There are times when we feel assured of being loved and other times less so, but either way, it doesn't hurt to be reminded. In fact, it helps in a number of important ways. Hearing our partner say "I love you" softens bad feelings and makes us more receptive to his advances. Telling our mate that we love him reassures him that he's being a good partner and reminds him that he's still our number one squeeze. I promise, if you say—and mean—I love you, every single day, your relationship will improve markedly in both tangible and intangible ways.

Of course, we don't always feel loving, which is another reason why we don't say the words. When we're angry, frustrated, or fed up with our partner, we may not, at that particular moment, be able to say I love you with any degree of sincerity. But here's the deal: We still love him, and he still loves us. We may not like his particular behavior, but that doesn't mean we've stopped loving him. Just as when our child misbehaves we say, "I love you, but I don't like how you are acting right now," we can disapprove of our partner's behavior and still acknowledge our love, without giving him a mixed message. We may also fail to say I love you because we're just not the "mushy type." Fair enough. We don't all have to turn into sentimental slobs; what matters is to say these words enough for your partner to truly know that you're aware of and expressing your love. Personally, I'm not one of those people who want to hear "I love you" every five minutes. I'd much rather be moved by less frequent but more intense statements of love inspired by those rare, perfect moments of ecstasy and transcendence.

We may also stumble over these words because of our upbringing. *If our family wasn't especially demonstrative, we may find it foreign and uncomfortable to say "I love you."* This just means it's time to learn something new. You needn't change your essential nature, personality, or values to tell your partner how much you love him or her. This is simple. It takes neither years of therapy nor months of practice; all that's required is paying attention and making an effort to verbally express your love.

Although women may not say "I love you" enough, we still tend to say it more than men do. We want and need to hear it back, and when we don't, we feel neglected and insecure about the status of our relationship. This presents a bit of a quandary, in that we don't really want to tell him to say "I love you" under duress—what good is it if we have to remind him? We can keep saying it, hoping he'll say it back, but we don't just want him to parrot us.

What we want is for him to be so in love with us that the words simply drip from his tongue. Okay, maybe that's going a little too far, but we certainly want our partner to feel enough love to say the words spontaneously, sincerely, and for no other reason than the best reason of all—he loves us.

The absence of these words, especially over a long period of time, creates a certain emptiness inside and estrangement within our relationship. When we treat each other as roommates, business partners, or coparents, at the expense of being romantic lovers, something is lost. Our relationship becomes more mechanical, more matter of fact, instead of our heart pounding when our partner walks through the door. Now, naturally, when we've been married for fifteen years, have two or three kids, and a volume of history between us, passion ebbs and flows, and that "wild heartbeat" we experienced early on is far less frequent. That's to be expected. And that's why we have to make an extra effort to put more passion, romance, and tenderness back into our relationship. Without it, we feel less and less like lovers, which we may resign ourselves to, but which is a real loss when you consider that being in love was what brought us together in the first place. In fact, the sharp contrast between the romance we may have felt in the beginning and what we have today is what makes it so hard for women to stop wanting to hear "I love you" from their mate.

WHAT HOOKS US

I don't care how many women tell me they want their mate to be their friend, companion, or source of support; I'm still convinced that every woman, to some degree or another, longs for a love affair with her mate. Write me if I'm wrong. Maybe I'm the last of the great romantics. Despite enough relationship pain to last a lifetime, I'm still holding out for the love affair of the century.

Friendship is crucial to the long-term survival of an intimate relationship. So are camaraderie, trust, rapport, shared goals, and the ability to coparent, (whether it's a kid or a cat). But without at least occasional moments of romance and passion, relationships go flat, which is what couples mean when they say "the magic is gone."

We can prevent the magic from disappearing by trying many of the strategies discussed in this book. But the single, most essential ingredient is our ability to feel and express our love to each other. How do we do this, especially if we're out of practice or not feeling particularly loving and romantic?

SIMPLE SOLUTIONS

Here's how: JUST DO IT! You've heard the saying "Fake it till you make it"? That's exactly what we need to do. Saying "I love you" when you're not feeling particularly loving isn't lying or putting on a pretense. It's a positive act that has the power to change how you feel, and how your partner feels in your relationship.

Here's how it works: Your relationship is in the doldrums. You're sitting at the kitchen table eating leftover meatloaf, talking about the weather, and feeling heartsick at how far apart you've grown. You sigh, stand up to clear the dishes, and as you reach over your partner's shoulder to pick up his spoon, you stop, stroke his hair, and say, "I love you," before heading toward the kitchen.

He may be surprised, suspicious, caught off guard, or enchanted by your gesture. He certainly won't shrug it off, especially if he hasn't heard these words for a while. He may do one of the following: Smile to himself and let it sink in without saying anything at all. Follow you into the kitchen and start drying the dishes. Ask you why you suddenly felt moved to say "I love you," or take you in his arms, kiss you sweetly, and say just what you want to hear.

Hey, it's worth a try! It may be just the right move to soften tensions and reawaken romance in your relationship. It may also involve a few risks. You risk his acting like it never happened, which may make you feel like an idiot. You risk the possibility of provoking a "what's wrong with our relationship" conversation, and mostly, you risk the pain of his not being able or willing to say "I love you" back. But then, love is full of risks, and this one's worth taking.

While simply saying "I love you" is the most important strategy, there are also ways of showing love, which we shouldn't overlook. Some people just can't or don't say "I love you" enough or at all, but are constantly expressing their affection in other ways. If you or your partner fall into this category, it's especially important to NOTICE THE NONVERBAL WAYS LOVE IS COMMUNICATED. Be aware of how often your partner touches you in passing or compliments you on how you look, what you say, or what you do. Be conscious of his efforts to court and seduce you, both in and out of bed. Every loving gesture, large or small, whether it's buying you your dream house or handing you lilacs, is a meaningful expression of love, which should be noted and appreciated.

Because that's what this is all about. Love and appreciation. GIVE MORE OF IT AND YOU WILL RECEIVE AT LEAST SOME OF IT IN RETURN. Whether your relationship remains the same, noticeably improves, or is dramatically transformed, remember that you still have the power to love and be loved.

Start now. Close the book, go to your partner, and tell him you love him. Then say it again. And again. And again.

ON THE BRIGHT SIDE

You now know the simple secrets of how to improve your relationship. Experiment. Do what works. Do it so that no matter what happens, you will always know in your heart that you have given everything you've got to making your relationship everything it can be.

AFTERWORD

True confession: I started writing this book shortly after ending a two-year relationship with a man I dearly loved and with whom I hoped to share the rest of my life. My heart was broken, my hope was shattered, and my optimism was at an all-time low. I definitely wasn't inspired; in fact, I was skeptical as to whether any lasting solutions to male-female conflicts even exist. But the book was due, and as usual, fate intervened.

As I sat before my computer, each chapter slowly unfolding before me, I began to see men through a different lens. My perspective had changed, perhaps as a result of having ended my relationship. I was no longer enraged nor drowning in despair. Having shed rivers of tears, having vented my rage at my ex-lover, I found myself in an interesting new place. Had I written this book while I was still madly in love, I think I would have been too mushy to have the necessary clarity and detachment. Had I still been in the early throes of my heartbreak, my anger would have poisoned my ability to have anything positive to say. So the timing was perfect.

For the first time since age seventeen, I wasn't involved with a man. I'd always gone from relationship to relationship. Instead of taking time to reflect and heal my wounds, I would immediately immerse myself in another love affair. Being alone gave me an entirely new perspective. Not being in the thick of a relationship left me feeling freer to explore new strategies. Not having a partner enabled me to have a clearer understanding of why men are the way they are, and being alone, without a man to blame for anything and everything that went wrong, forced me to honestly examine why women are the way we are!

I've chosen the most universal issues women have with men, based both on my personal experience and on my extensive professional contact with women from all walks of life. As I tried to find answers to each question, I found many of my own questions answered. I came to strongly believe that relationships have become too complicated, that we need to take a less serious, more lighthearted approach. I realized the need for practical, hands-on strategies for solving relationship problems rather than spending twenty years and thousands of dollars in therapy. I've learned that there are simpler solutions if we truly understand how men work and are open to trying innovative strategies to get what we want out of our relationship.

So the truth is, although I wrote this book in an effort to help you, in the end I helped myself. I guess that's why they call these books "self-help." My heart has mended, my hope is restored, and I am convinced more than ever before that it is possible to create a healthy, loving relationship with a man. Having reached the final page of this book, I hope that reading it has led you to a similar conclusion. If it has, I will feel gratified because, when all is said and done, I still believe that love is the greatest force in the universe. May this book bring more love into your life and inspire you to be more loving toward others.